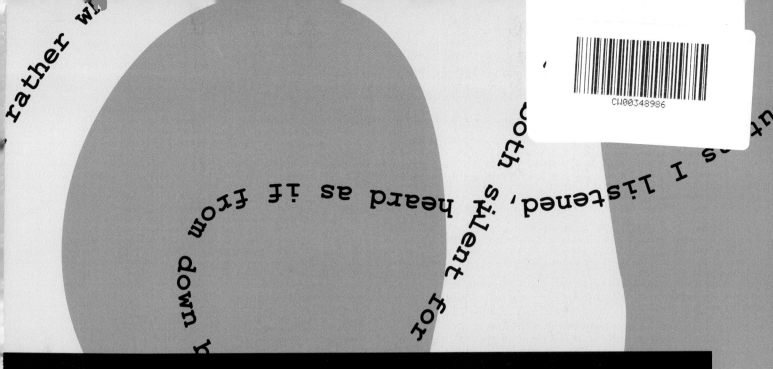

Skills for Writing

Units 3 and 4

David Grant
Series consultant: Debra Myhill

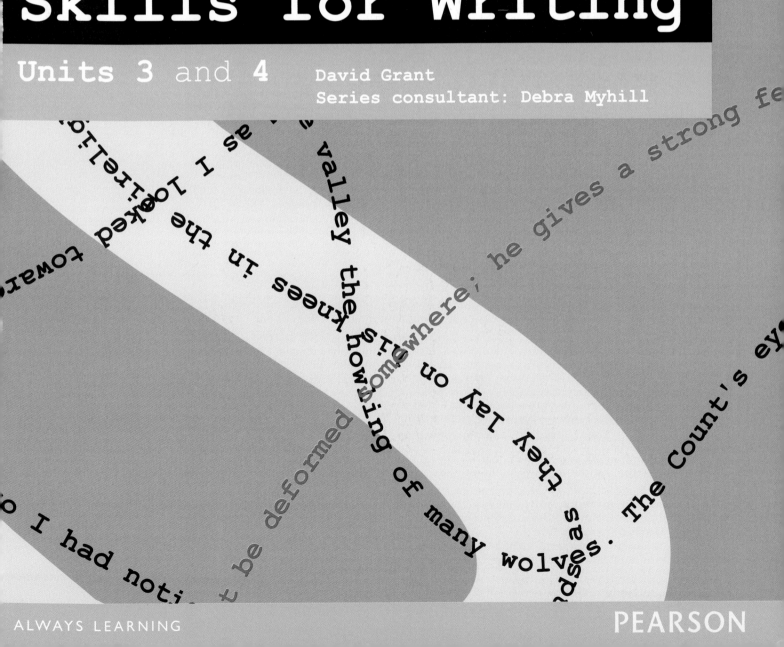

CW00348986

ALWAYS LEARNING

PEARSON

Published by Pearson Education Limited, Edinburgh Gate, Harlow, Essex, CM20 2JE.

www.pearsonschoolsandfecolleges.co.uk

Text © Pearson Education Limited 2014
Typeset by Jerry Udall and Tek-Art
The right of David Grant to be identified as author of this work has been asserted by him in accordance with the Copyright, Designs and Patents Act 1988.

First published 2014

16 15 14
10 9 8 7 6 5 4 3 2 1

British Library Cataloguing in Publication Data
A catalogue record for this book is available from the British Library

ISBN 9781447948766

Copyright notice

All rights reserved. No part of this publication may be reproduced in any form or by any means (including photocopying or storing it in any medium by electronic means and whether or not transiently or incidentally to some other use of this publication) without the written permission of the copyright owner, except in accordance with the provisions of the Copyright, Designs and Patents Act 1988 or under the terms of a licence issued by the Copyright Licensing Agency, Saffron House, 6–10 Kirby Street, London EC1N 8TS (www. cla.co.uk). Applications for the copyright owner's written permission should be addressed to the publisher.

Printed in Italy by Lego S.p.a

Acknowledgements

We would like to thank Debra Myhill at the University of Exeter for her invaluable help in the development of this course.

The author and publisher would like to thank the following individuals and organisations for permission to reproduce photographs:

(Key: b-bottom; c-centre; l-left; r-right; t-top)

Alamy Images: Everett Collection Historical 3, LOOK Die Bildagentur der Fotografen GmbH 23, Moviestore Collection 4 (Bourne Identity), 44bl, Paul Carstairs 36, Pictorial Press 41t; J H Photo 50br, Jane Hobson 65, John Angerson 86br, Nick Gregory 66, Paul Gapper 59, 61, Peter M Wilson 69, Robert Harding Picture Library 51, Stacey Walsh Rosenstock 86bl, Zuma Press Inc 53; BBC Photo Library: © Endor Productions; Hayley Atwell as Eva Delectorskaya and Rufus Sewell as Lucas Rover 39; Corbis: Peter Steffen / epa 47 (UO), 83, Getty Images: Julian Hibbard 41b, Nomadic Images 35, Peter Hince 24, Ryan McVay 29; Getty. 76, 77, 86tl; James Davies: 56; Knaresborough Lions Club: 62, 64; Penguin Books Ltd: 8, 22, 32, 38, 44tc, 44tr, 44bc; Photos.com: Ablestock.com 31t, Denis Jr. Tangney 31c, Hemera Technologies 9, 40t, Jupiter Images 40b, Morten Lau-Nielsen 28, Thinkstock 30, Zastockphotos 7l; Press Association Images: Johnny Green 49; Reuters: Darren Staples 86tr; Rex Features: Moviestore Collection 15; Shutterstock. com: 100079606 vi, oksana2010 84, RTImages 48, Tulpahn 73, YanLev i; The Kobal Collection: Danjaq / Eon Productions 41r, EON / Danaq / Sony 2 (James Bond), 18, 19 (James Bond), Paramount 2 (Mission Impossible), 19 (Mission Impossible), Universal 2 (Jason Bourne), 6, 19 (Bourne), Weinstein 2 (Alex Rider), 4 (Stormbreaker); The Random House Group Ltd.: 4 (Moonraker), 44tl; Veer/Corbis: BestPhotoStudio 14, lokes 16Csaba Vanyi 78, 85, Norman Chan 50bl, Tom Gowanlock 50tr

All other images © Pearson Education

We are grateful to the following for permission to reproduce copyright material:

Figures
Pages 52-53 from "The 6 stack" diagram. Reproduced with kind permission of Speed Stacks, Inc. www.speedstacks.com;

Text
Extract page 6 from *The Bourne Imperative*, Orion (Robert Ludlum and Eric Van Lustbader 2012) pp.1-2, ISBN 9781409116455; Extract pages 8-9. from *Hurricane Gold*, Penguin (Charlie Higson 2012) pp.59-60, copyright ©Ian Fleming Publications Ltd, 2007, www.ianfleming. com, reproduced with permission of Ian Fleming Publications Ltd, London; Extract page 12 from *Alex Rider: Scorpia*, Walker Books (Anthony Horowitz 2005) pp.11-12, ISBN 0744570514, text © 2004 Stormbreaker Productions, Trademarks Alex Rider™, Boy with Torch Logo™ © 2010 Stormbreaker Productions Ltd, reproduced by permission of Walker Books Ltd, London SE11 5HJ; www.walker.co.uk; Extract page 16 from *Alex Rider: Scorpia Rising*, Walker Books (Anthony Horowitz 2011) pp14-17, ISBN 978-1406 310498, reproduced by permission of Walker Books Ltd; Extract pages 22-23 and page 29 from *Devil May Care* by Sebastian Faulks writing as Ian Fleming (Penguin 007, 2008, Penguin Books 2009), copyright © Ian Fleming Publications, 2008.; Extract page 32 from *The Hidden Man*, Penguin (Charles Cumming 2006) pp.3-4, reprinted by permission of HarperCollins Publishers Ltd, copyright © 2006, Charles Cumming; Extract page 38 from *Restless, TV Tie in edition*, Bloomsbury Publishing Plc (William Boyd 2012) p.22, copyright © William Boyd, 2012; Extract page 48 from "Top 10 Facts about balls", *The Daily Express*, 18/07/2013 (William Hartston), www.express.co.uk copyright © Express Newspapers; Extract page 56 adapted from 'History of sport stacking' www.speedstacks.com/instructors/resources/history/ reproduced with kind permission of Speed Stacks, Inc.; Extract page 58 adapted from "Things you never knew about Worm Charming!" by Gordon Farr and Mike Forster,http://www.wormcharming.com/facts.html#.Ukwalla-2ul, copyright © IFCWAP 2002-2013; Extract page 70 from *BTEC Level 3 National Sport Book 2*, Edexcel (Ray Barker et al 2010) text copyright © Pearson Education Limited, 2010; Extract page 76 from "Have you got the bug for bunnies?" *The Telegraph*, 05/04/2012 (Jake Wallis Simons), copyright © Telegraph Media Group Limited; Extract page 82 from "We could be heroes", *The Guardian*, 13/12/2003 (Myles Quin), copyright © Guardian Nerws & Media Ltd 2003.

Every effort has been made to contact copyright holders of material reproduced in this book. Any omissions will be rectified in subsequent printings if notice is given to the publishers.

Contents

Skills for Writing

Skills for Writing is a unique digital, print and training solution. Developed in partnership with Professor Debra Myhill and her team from the University of Exeter, it embeds the principles of the Grammar for Writing pedagogy – trialled and proven to accelerate the rate of writing progress significantly.

ActiveTeach: interactive front-of-class teaching

ActiveTeach Presentation is our digital front-of-class teaching tool, providing you with the book on-screen and a wealth of additional interactive resources to help you embed the Grammar for Writing pedagogy.

Real text extracts introduce students to the choices that authors make in order to create certain effects in their writing.

The Writer's Workshop area guides students through the grammatical choices writers make and the effects they create.

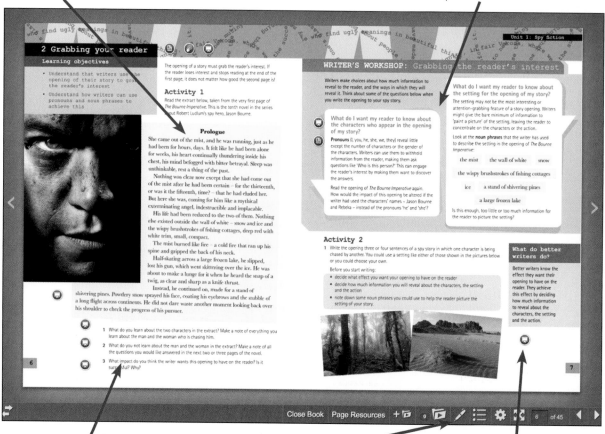

Each page is divided into zoom areas, allowing you to enlarge and annotate each section using the annotation tool.

The annotation tool can be used to identify effective use of language and to record students' responses to an extract.

Hotspot icons link to resources for each lesson, including PowerPoints, worksheets, videos and interactive activities.

Teacher guide

The lesson plans in the teacher guide take you through all you need to teach a Skills for Writing lesson. The lessons guide you through the activities in the student book explaining the effect that is being focused on, providing additional support on the grammatical concepts covered and referring to the relevant resources from ActiveTeach. Extra activities for students needing more support or challenge are also suggested in every lesson plan – ideal for differentiating the learning.

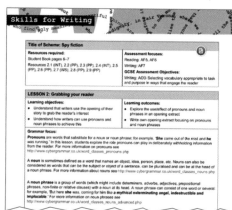

ActiveLearn: online, independent learning

ActiveLearn includes **ActiveBooks** and an **ActiveCourse** that provides your students with a range of independent digital learning exercises for completion as homework. Linking closely to the learning focus of the in-class teaching, these exercises are carefully designed to consolidate and boost understanding and to motivate students to become more independent learners and writers.

Digital homework activities allow students to consolidate and test their understanding of the grammar features that have been focused on in class.

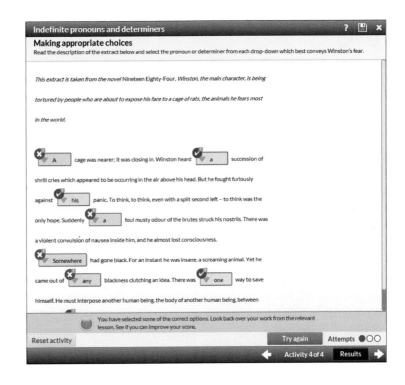

Students are given three attempts at each activity, with hints and tips to motivate them after each attempt.

Independent writing activities encourage students to practise writing and then to reflect on the language choices they have made.

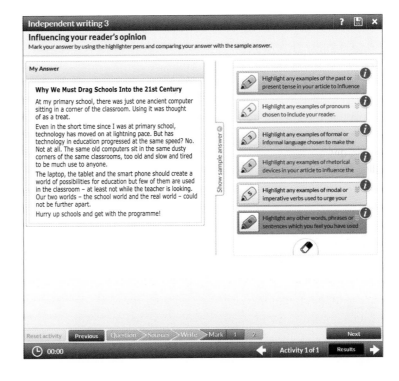

ActiveLearn also provides you with detailed reporting on how students are performing, enabling you to track and monitor progress in writing.

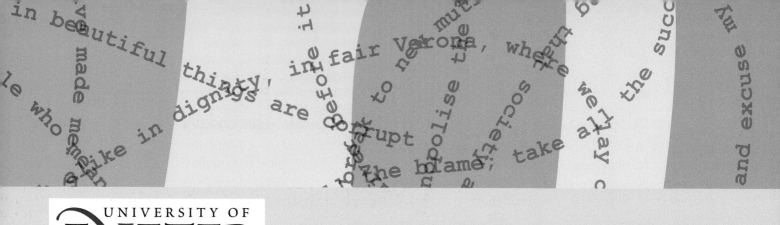

UNIVERSITY OF
EXETER

Learning to write is about learning to be powerful. When you can write confidently, you can make things happen: you can campaign for things that matter to you; you can present yourself and your personality in writing for job or university applications; you can express your deepest, most personal feelings; you can write stories and poems that make others laugh or weep. In fact, you can write to change the world!

This book is to help you become a confident, powerful writer. It sets out to show you how authors create and convey different meanings in their writing by the choices they make, and invites you to consider how the meaning might have been subtly different had they made different choices. The book is very clear about how you can become a better writer, but it is not a recipe book or set of instructions for success. Writing is far more complex than that. We want you to think like a writer, knowing what choices and possibilities you have in each piece of writing, and being able to make and justify those choices with confidence. Enjoy the power!

Debra Myhill

Unit 3

Spy fiction

In this unit you will explore the elements that make an engaging spy story. You will learn how to submerse your reader in a world of mystery, action and danger and create realistic characters who jump off the page. You will write extracts of your own spy story in which your hero takes on a secret mission, encounters a villain face-to-face, gets into a sticky situation and has words with his boss. Finally, you will write your own complete short spy story, planning the plot, choosing the setting and drawing on all the language skills you have built up in order to entertain and thrill everyone who reads it.

1 Going undercover

- Understand the key features of the spy fiction genre and how they engage the reader
- Understand how writers use narrative structure to engage the reader
- Understand how to use narrative structure to plan a story

The secret lives of spies have fascinated readers and film audiences for decades. Spy stories often share similar ingredients.

Activity 1

Look at the jumbled words below. Your mission is to decipher some key ingredients of an effective spy story. You will use these to plan your own spy story.

orshee	svanilli	rotateironing	crestes
githfing	gasten	desoc	adreng

Activity 2

1 How many of the spies and spy stories above do you recognise? Can you think of any well-known fictional spies? Write down what you know about each one in a table like the one below:

Name of spy	What I know about them
James Bond	Known as 007, works with M

2 Imagine you are the head of the secret service. You are hoping to recruit a new spy. What qualities should a good spy have? Make a list like this:

The perfect spy should be:
- *brave*
- *intelligent*

Activity 3

Stories and films in the spy genre share some key ingredients. These are what make them a spy story.

1 Look at the different ingredients below. Which of these ingredients do you think a good spy story:

- MUST have?   • COULD have?   • SHOULD NOT have?

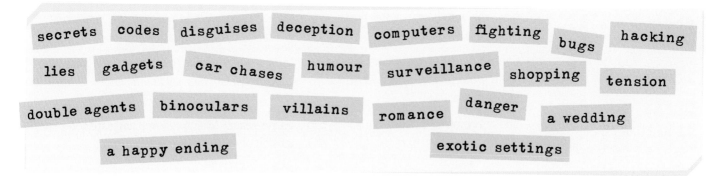

secrets   codes   disguises   deception   computers   fighting   bugs   hacking

lies   gadgets   car chases   humour   surveillance   shopping   tension

double agents   binoculars   villains   romance   danger   a wedding

a happy ending   exotic settings

Use a table like the one below to organise your ideas:

A good spy story MUST have	A good spy story COULD have	A good spy story SHOULD NOT have

2 Look at the information below about real-life spy Fritz Joubert Duquesne. Do you think it would make an exciting, engaging book or film? What ingredients does it have that would make it an effective spy story?

Fritz Joubert Duquesne

- Born South Africa 1877
- Described as handsome, charming, fluent in several languages
- Joined South African army 1899; fought against and imprisoned by the British. Escaped by seducing prison guard's daughter
- Joined British army 1901 so he could return to war in South Africa and sabotage British
- Caught trying to kill British leader General Kitchener and imprisoned. Avoided death penalty by giving away South African army's secret codes (they were fakes)
- Escaped from prison, travelled to America, became spy for Germany in World War I, sabotaging British ships with bombs disguised as cargo
- Caught and imprisoned, faked paralysis for 2 years so he would be sent to prison hospital
- Escaped from prison hospital by cutting through bars of cell and scaling prison's walls dressed as a woman
- Disappeared for nearly 20 years
- Arrested by FBI in 1941 for leading a spy ring that had been giving secret information to Nazis since World War II started in 1939
- Imprisoned 1941-54
- Died 1956

3

Stories (and films) are structured to engage the reader (or viewer). This structure can be simplified into four basic stages:

	What does it mean?	What effect does it have?
1 Exposition	Setting, characters and situation introduced	Gives reader enough information to engage them in story; makes them wonder how it will develop
2 Conflict	Main character(s) encounter problem they must overcome	Makes reader want to find out how characters will tackle difficult situation
3 Climax	Conflict reaches worst point; it's not just a problem now – it's a REALLY SERIOUS problem	Leaves reader unable to work out how main character(s) can ever solve problem
4 Resolution	Conflict resolved – happily or sadly	Leaves reader feeling relieved and satisfied that tension of story has come to an end

Activity 4

1   Look at the summaries of the spy stories below. Identify the four stages of each story.
    You could write your ideas in a table like the one at the top of the next page.

Moonraker

Hugo Drax owns a company that is building the first British nuclear missile. The British secret service suspects Drax of foul play and assigns secret agent **James Bond** to investigate. Bond discovers that Drax intends to use the missile to destroy London. As Drax is about to launch the missile, Bond resets the coordinates, sending the missile into the sea, where it kills Drax, who is attempting to escape by submarine.

Stormbreaker

Alex Rider is told that his uncle has been killed in a car crash. Alex suspects this is untrue and, on a visit to the bank where his uncle worked, sneaks into his office. Alex is caught and learns that his uncle was a spy for MI6 – and that he must

take over his last mission, investigating the multimillionaire, Herod Sayle. Sayle is developing a new computer system called Stormbreaker and plans to donate one to every school in the UK. Alex is trained as an MI6 agent and sent to Sayle's production plant. Alex discovers that Sayle will use the computers to spread an epidemic of smallpox. Sayle tries to kill Alex but Alex escapes and manages to foil Sayle's plot with seconds to spare.

The Bourne Identity

A man wakes up suffering from amnesia. He learns that he was found floating in the sea with gunshot wounds, has had plastic surgery to hide his identity, and had the details of a secret bank account implanted in his body. The man discovers his name is **Jason Bourne** and that he worked for an organisation linked to the CIA. Bourne travels around France and America, trying to discover his true identity while fighting off a dangerous terrorist called Carlos. Eventually Bourne defeats Carlos' men and discovers the truth about himself...

Use a table like the one below to record the four stages of each story:

	Moonraker	The Bourne Identity	Stormbreaker
1 Exposition			
2 Conflict			

2   Use your answers to question 1 to compare the three stories. Make a note of some of the similarities and some of the differences. For example:

> • A similarity: The villains are defeated in the resolutions of 'Stormbreaker' and 'Moonraker'.

Activity 5

Look at your answers to all the activities in this unit so far. Use them to plan the plot of your own spy story.

1   Think about the hero of your story. Who are they? Male or female? How did they become a spy? What makes them a good spy?

2   Plan the four different stages of your story: exposition, conflict, climax and resolution.

3   Look back at some of the key ingredients of spy stories you identified in Activity 3. What other key ingredients would make your spy story really effective? Add them to your plan.

What do better writers do?

Better writers:

• use the key features of their chosen genre, but avoid directly copying ideas

• plan their stories, thinking about the effect they want each stage to have on the reader

• keep their readers guessing – exactly HOW will the hero defeat the villain, for example?

CHECK YOUR WRITING

➡ Look back at your story planning in Activity 5. What effect do you want each stage of your story to have on the reader? Annotate your plan, explaining the effect you want it to have and how you think it will achieve this.

⬇ Which column in the table below do you think best describes your planning?

I can plan a spy story using the four-part story structure of exposition, conflict, climax, resolution.	I can plan a spy story using the four-part story structure, developing some of my ideas in detail.	I can use my own ideas to plan an original spy story using the four-part story structure, developing most of my ideas in detail.
I have used some of the key ingredients of the genre, thinking about the effect some of them will have on the reader.	I have used a range of the genre's key ingredients, thinking about how they will grab and hold the reader's interest.	I have selected a variety of the genre's key ingredients by carefully considering the effect they will have on the reader.

5

2 Grabbing your reader

Learning objectives

- Understand that writers use the opening of their story to grab the reader's interest
- Understand how writers can use personal pronouns, determiners and noun phrases to achieve this

The opening of a story must grab the reader's interest. If the reader loses interest and stops reading at the end of the first page, it does not matter how good the second page is!

Activity 1

Read the extract below, taken from the very first page of *The Bourne Imperative*. This is the tenth novel in the series about Robert Ludlum's spy hero, Jason Bourne.

Prologue

She came out of the mist, and he was running, just as he had been for hours, days. It felt like he had been alone for weeks, his heart continually thundering inside his chest, his mind befogged with bitter betrayal. Sleep was unthinkable, rest a thing of the past.

Nothing was clear now except that she had come out of the mist after he had been certain – for the thirteenth, or was it the fifteenth, time? – that he had eluded her. But here she was, coming for him like a mythical exterminating angel, indestructible and implacable.

His life had been reduced to the two of them. Nothing else existed outside the wall of white – snow and ice and the wispy brushstrokes of fishing cottages, deep red with white trim, small, compact.

The mist burned like fire – a cold fire that ran up his spine and gripped the back of his neck.

Half-skating across a large frozen lake, he slipped, lost his gun, which went skittering over the ice. He was about to make a lunge for it when he heard the snap of a twig, as clear and sharp as a knife thrust.

Instead, he continued on, made for a stand of shivering pines. Powdery snow sprayed his face, coating his eyebrows and the stubble of a long flight across continents. He did not dare waste another moment looking back over his shoulder to check the progress of his pursuer.

1 What do you learn about the two characters in the extract? Make a note of everything you learn about the man and the woman who is chasing him.

2 What do you not learn about the man and the woman in the extract? Make a note of all the questions you would like answered in the next two or three pages of the novel.

3 What impact do you think the writer wants this opening to have on the reader? Is it successful? Why?

WRITER'S WORKSHOP: Grabbing the reader's interest

Writers make choices about how much information to reveal to the reader, and the ways in which they will reveal it. Think about some of the questions below when you write the opening to your spy story.

What do I want my reader to know about the characters who appear in the opening of my story?

Personal pronouns (I, you, he, she, we, they) and **related determiners** (my, your, his, her, our, their) reveal little except the number of characters or the gender of the characters. Writers can use them to withhold information from the reader, making them ask questions like 'Who is this person?' This can engage the reader's interest by making them want to discover the answers.

Read the opening of *The Bourne Imperative* again. How would the impact of this opening be altered if the writer had used the characters' names – Jason Bourne and Rebeka – instead of the pronouns 'he' and 'she'?

What do I want my reader to know about the setting for the opening of my story?

The setting may not be the most interesting or attention-grabbing feature of a story opening. Writers might give the bare minimum of information to 'paint a picture' of the setting, leaving the reader to concentrate on the characters or the action.

Look at the nouns and **noun phrases** that the writer has used to describe the setting in the opening of *The Bourne Imperative*:

the mist	the wall of white	snow

the wispy brushstrokes of fishing cottages

ice	a stand of shivering pines

a large frozen lake

Is this enough, too little or too much information for the reader to picture the setting?

Activity 2

1   Write the opening three or four sentences of a spy story in which one character is being chased by another. You could use a setting like either of those shown in the pictures below or you could choose your own.

Before you start writing:

- decide what effect you want your opening to have on the reader
- decide how much information you will reveal about the characters, the setting and the action
- note down some noun phrases you could use to help the reader picture the setting of your story.

What do better writers do?

Better writers know the effect they want their opening to have on the reader. They achieve this effect by deciding how much information to reveal about the characters, the setting and the action.

3 Pace and threat

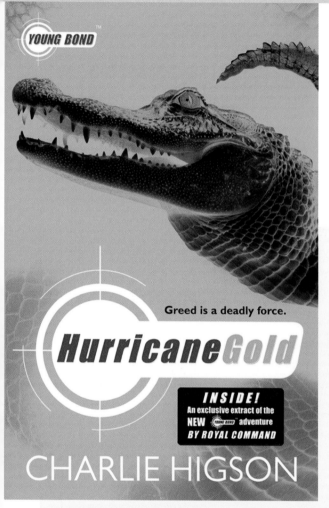

Greed is a deadly force.

Hurricane Gold

INSIDE!
An exclusive extract of the
NEW YOUNG BOND adventure
BY ROYAL COMMAND

CHARLIE HIGSON

Pace and threat are two of the key elements of a successful spy story. The hero is constantly placed in dangerous and threatening situations – and often, as soon as they escape from one dangerous and threatening situation, they find themselves in another! Writers use this high level of pace and threat to hold the reader's attention.

Activity 1

Read the extract below, taken from the fourth novel in the Young Bond series, *Hurricane Gold*.

Young James Bond is visiting Jack Stone's house in Mexico with his aunt. Gangsters have broken into the house to steal Stone's gold. The gangsters are pressurising his children, Precious and JJ, to tell them where the gold is hidden but a tropical storm is on its way...

James watched as the young man waved his gun at Precious and JJ.

'Where's your father?' he yelled. 'Tell me or I'll hurt you.'

'He's not here,' wailed Precious. 'He's flown down south. He won't be back until after the storm.'

As Precious said the word 'storm' three things happened at once. There was a terrific crack of thunder, the whole house shook and the lights went out.

The storm had finally arrived.

Precious screamed. The young man snarled at her to shut up. There was just enough light coming through the window for James to see him grab the two children and drag them out of the room.

James stayed put, breathing heavily. The intruders seemed to have come prepared, but with luck they wouldn't know that he was here at all.

James waited in the Wendy house for a full five minutes. Once he was sure that the man wasn't coming back he crept out of his hiding place and tiptoed over to the playroom door.

He hardly needed to be quiet. The storm was making a fearsome racket as it buffeted the house. There was a cacophony of different sounds; crashing, hissing, roaring, squealing, rumbling.

As he moved out into the corridor James felt the full force of the wind slam into the house like a physical object. He could actually feel the floor moving beneath his feet, and the walls seemed to sway and shudder. He glanced out of the window, but all he could see was a swirling maelstrom of cloud and rain. There was a startling flash and another blast of thunder, then a gust of wind so powerful it blew the windows in. The rain followed, hosing down the corridor in horizontal bars. The walls were instantly soaked and a picture flew off the wall.

The noise from outside was like nothing that James had ever heard before, like boulders crashing down a mountainside. The wind was whipping around in the corridor and the house was vibrating as if at any moment it might crack up and be blown away.

James dropped to his knees and crawled along the sodden carpet as bits of debris were hurled past his head.

He reached the stairs and slid down them on his backside in the darkness. He made it safely to the lower landing and peered out between the banisters into the hallway below.

The servants were being rounded up and herded into the dining room by two of the men. The raid had been planned like a military operation.

James was the only person who might be able to get out and go for help.

1 In this extract, James, Precious and JJ face two different threats at the same time. What are they?

2 What impressions do you get of these two different threats?

   a Write down two or three words or phrases to describe each of these two threats.

   b Try to identify *how* the writer has given you these impressions.

3 Look at the final sentence of the extract.

   James was the only person who might be able to get out and go for help.

What does this suggest about:

   a the character of James Bond?

   b the role of the hero in spy stories?

9

WRITER'S WORKSHOP: Creating a sense of pace and threat

How can I choose language to create a sense of threat?

Writers can create a sense of threat through the details they choose to describe, but they can increase the sense of threat through the language they use to describe those details.

Look at the **verbs** the writer has used to describe what one of the gangsters says and does:

'Where's your father?' he yelled.
'Tell me or I'll hurt you.'

Precious screamed. The young man snarled at her to shut up. There was just enough light coming through the window for James to see him grab the two children and drag them out of the room.

Now look at the **verbs** the writer has chosen to describe the impact of the storm:

James felt the full force of the wind slam into the house like a physical object. He could actually feel the floor moving beneath his feet, and the walls seemed to sway and shudder.

How effective are these verbs? Try replacing each one with a new verb to add to the sense of threat.

For example, what is the effect of changing:

'Where's your father?' he yelled.   to   'Where's your father?' he moaned.

or   'Where's your father?' he asked.

How can I use paragraphs to create pace in my narrative?

There are four reasons to start a new paragraph in your writing:

* when you change the subject or focus of your story
* when you change to a new setting
* when you change to a new time
* when a different character begins speaking.

However, writers often ignore these rules when they want to create a sense of pace. In the Young Bond extract, the writer has used lots of short paragraphs as he quickly moves his focus from the gangsters to the storm to James Bond's movements through the house.

Look at the shortest paragraph in the extract: The storm had finally arrived.

The writer has isolated this sentence in its own, very short paragraph to give this moment more dramatic impact and heighten the threat of the storm.

Are there any other sentences in the extract that would make an effective short paragraph?

Activity 2

1 Look again at the story you planned in Activity 5 on page 5. Choose a section of your story where you think you could create a sense of pace and threat to hold the reader's attention. It could be:

- your hero is being threatened by a villain or villains, like the gangsters in the Young Bond extract
- your hero is being threatened by a difficult or dangerous situation, like the storm in the Young Bond extract
- something else.

2 **a** Make a list of verbs you could use to emphasise the threat in your story. The verbs could describe the way a character speaks, the way a character acts, the situation your hero is in, etc.

b When making this list, you could think about some of the verbs used in the texts you have read so far in this unit.

yelled	running	lunge	shudder	skittering
snarled	thundering	slam	eluded	shivering
grab	slipped	sway	burned	sprayed

3 Write a short extract from this part of your story. Aim to write five to ten sentences using the verbs you have thought of in appropriate places to suggest danger, action or pace.

What do better writers do?

Better writers:

- are very aware of the effect they want to have on their reader
- choose vocabulary such as verbs very carefully to achieve this effect
- vary the lengths of their paragraphs, using longer paragraphs to convey information, and shorter paragraphs for dramatic impact.

CHECK YOUR WRITING

→ Look back at your writing from Activity 2. Annotate your extract to explain some of the decisions you have made. It might look something like this:

He hurtled through the trees, the jungle just a blur of green. He could hear them, hear their angry shouts as they smashed through the dense under-growth just metres behind him.

And then silence.

pronouns and determiners make reader wonder who these people are and what is going on

verb choices create a sense of movement and pace

short, one-sentence paragraph suggests a sudden, unexpected change

↓ Which column best describes your use of paragraphing and verb choice?

| I used some paragraphs to organise my main ideas. | I used paragraphs throughout and had some success with creating a sense of pace with my paragraphs. | I used paragraphs clearly and effectively throughout to give my story a sense of pace. |
| I chose some verbs deliberately, but some verb choices did not contribute to the sense of threat. | Most of my verb choices were deliberate and contributed to the sense of threat. | I chose all of my verbs carefully and deliberately to create a sense of pace and threat. |

11

4 Narrative viewpoint

Learning objectives

- Understand what is meant by narrative viewpoint
- Understand the impact that the writer's choice of narrative viewpoint can have on a text

One of the key decisions writers must make is about who they will use to tell their story. There are a lot of different ways in which stories can be told – and each one will affect how the reader responds to it.

Activity 1

Read the extract below. It is from *Scorpia*, the fifth book in the Alex Rider series by Anthony Horowitz.

Alex knew very little about his mother and father, John and Helen Rider. In his bedroom he had a photo of them: a watchful, handsome man with close-cut hair standing with his arm around a pretty, half-smiling woman. He had been in the army and still looked like a soldier. She had been a nurse, working in radiology. But they were strangers to him; he couldn't remember anything about them. They had died while he was still a baby. In a plane crash. That was what he had been told.

Now he knew otherwise.

The plane crash had been as much a lie as his uncle's car accident. Yassen Gregorovich had told him the truth on Air Force One. Alex's father had been an assassin – just like Yassen. The two of them had even worked together: John Rider had once saved Yassen's life. But then his father had been killed by MI6 – the very same people who had forced Alex to work for them three times, lying to him, manipulating him and finally dumping him when he was no longer needed. It was almost impossible to believe, but Yassen had offered him a way to find proof.

Go to Venice. Find Scorpia. And you will find your destiny...

Alex had to know what had happened fourteen years ago. Discovering the truth about John Rider would be the same as finding out about himself. Because, if his father really had killed people for money, what did that make him? Alex was angry, unhappy... and confused. He had to find Scorpia, whatever it was. Scorpia would tell him what he needed to know.

1 What do you learn about the characters in the extract? You could write your answers in a table like the one below.

Alex Rider	John Rider	Helen Rider	Yassen Gregorovich

2 Which character do you learn most about in the extract? Why do you think this is?

3 a Look again at your answer to question 1. What do you learn about each of the characters in terms of:
   - facts about their lives?
   - details about their appearance?
   - their thoughts?
   - their feelings?

   b Which of these things tells you the most about a character?

WRITER'S WORKSHOP: Deciding on narrative viewpoint

Before a writer starts writing a story, they must decide who will narrate it – from whose point of view the story will be told. This is called **narrative viewpoint**.

Do I want everything in my story to be told from one person's viewpoint?

The following extract is taken from *Epitaph for a Spy* by Eric Ambler, a story told by the main character:

> I was silent for a moment. There was something curious about the chemist's manner. His eyes, magnified by the thick pebble glasses he wore, remained fixed on mine. There was an odd look in them. Then I realised what the look was. The man was frightened.

This story is written in **first person narrative**. We are told everything that happens in the story from the point of view of a character in the story, using the pronouns 'I' and 'we'.

Choosing to write in **first person narrative** means:

- the writer can describe the main character's thoughts and feelings and point of view directly
- the reader may be more engaged with the story because they feel they are being told the story by someone who was there when it happened
- the writer cannot describe other characters' thoughts and feelings (such as the chemist's fear in the extract above) directly – the reader must learn about them through the first person narrator
- everything the writer wants the reader to see and hear must be seen and heard by the narrator.

13

Do I want my story to be told by a narrator who is not involved in the action?

Most spy stories are told using **third person narrative**. The story is told by a narrator using the pronouns 'he', 'she' and 'they'. The narrator does not take part in the action of the story – it's as though they are spying on the characters!

Look again at the example from *Scorpia*. The pronouns and related determiners have been highlighted. They show the story is being told by a third person narrator – someone outside the action of the story.

> Alex knew very little about his mother and father, John and Helen Rider. In his bedroom he had a photo of them: a watchful, handsome man with close-cut hair standing with his arm around a pretty, half-smiling woman.

Choosing to write in **third person narrative** means:

- the writer can describe all the different characters' thoughts and feelings – although, like Anthony Horowitz, they may decide to focus on the main character for most of the story
- the writer can describe events that the main character does not see or hear.

How do I choose?

Before deciding on the narrative viewpoint for your story, ask yourself the following questions:

> Will my main character be present at all the events I want to include in my story?

> Do I want to describe all the characters' thoughts and feelings directly ('She was angry'), or indirectly, through the eyes of the main character ('I thought she looked angry')?

> Will it be a more engaging story if the main character tells the reader directly about his or her experience?

What do better writers do?

Better writers think about the advantages and disadvantages of first and third person narrative and choose the narrative viewpoint that best suits the story they want to tell.

Activity 2

1 What would be the effect of changing the narrative viewpoint in the *Scorpia* extract on page 12?

   a Try rewriting the last paragraph in the **first person** from Alex's viewpoint.

   b What effect has this change of narrative viewpoint had? Write two or three sentences explaining your ideas.

2 What would be the effect of playing with the narrative viewpoint in the *Epitaph for a Spy* extract on page 13?

   a Try rewriting the paragraph in the **third person**.

   b What effect has this change of narrative viewpoint had? Write two or three sentences explaining your ideas.

Activity 3

Look at the image and script extract from the James Bond film *Goldfinger*.

Villainous super-criminal, Auric Goldfinger, has caught James Bond, tied him to a huge slab of gold and now watches as a laser slices through the gold, heading towards Bond.

BOND: Do you expect me to talk?
GOLDFINGER: No, Mr Bond, I expect you to die!

1 Write one or two paragraphs telling the story of this scene from the viewpoint of **James Bond**. Write your story in the **first person**.

2 Write one or two paragraphs telling the story of this scene from the viewpoint of **Goldfinger**. Write your story in the **first person**.

3 Write one or two paragraphs telling the story of this scene in the **third person**.

4 What difference do the different viewpoints make to the telling of the story? Which one do you think the writer should choose to tell this part of the story? Write two or three sentences explaining why.

5 Building character description

Learning objective

- Understand how to write vivid descriptions by expanding noun phrases using adjectives, adverbs and prepositional phrases

Villains are some of the most interesting and engaging characters in spy stories. An effective villain is not simply a character who puts the hero in danger. You also need to think about how they look and behave, why they are villains in the first place and whether they are villainous from head to toe.

Activity 1

Read this description of a spy story villain. It is from *Scorpia Rising*, the ninth book in the Alex Rider series by Anthony Horowitz.

His name was Zeljan Kurst and he was wanted by the police in seventeen different countries. He was the chief executive of the international criminal organization known as Scorpia and, as far as it was known, he had never been seen on the streets of London. However, MI6 had been tipped off that he was coming, and they had been waiting for him to land. The passport official was one of their secret agents. They were following him now…

Zeljan Kurst was a large man with heavy, broad shoulders that formed a straight line on either side of an unnaturally thick neck. He was bald by choice. His head had been shaved and there was a dark grey shadow beneath the skin. His eyes, a muddy brown, showed little intelligence and he had the thick lips and small, squashed nose of a wrestler, or perhaps a bouncer at a shady nightclub. Many people had underestimated him and occasionally Kurst had found it necessary to correct them. This usually involved killing them.

1 Look closely at the first paragraph of description. What do you learn about the character of Zeljan Kurst?

2 Now look closely at the second paragraph of description.

   a What is Anthony Horowitz suggesting about the character of Zeljan Kurst?

   b Write a sentence or two commenting on what each of these quotations suggests:

a large man with heavy, broad shoulders

Many people had underestimated him

he had the thick lips and small, squashed nose of a wrestler, or perhaps a bouncer at a shady nightclub

there was a dark grey shadow beneath the skin

This usually involved killing them.

3 Which tells you more about the character – the description of who he is and what he does in the first paragraph, or the description of his appearance and actions in the second paragraph?

WRITER'S WORKSHOP: Creating effective characters

To create an engaging spy story, writers need to create interesting characters – and one of the most important characters in this genre is the villain.

What language choices will help me add effective detail about characters?

Writers can add detail and depth to character descriptions with carefully chosen **adjectives**, **adverbs** or **prepositional phrases**. These are some of the choices you can make:

a You could use **adjectives** (words that add descriptive information to nouns) to form noun phrases:

a large man   ▢ adjective   ▢ noun

b You could use an **adverb** (adverbs can add descriptive information to adjectives) to **pre-modify** your chosen **adjective**:

an unnaturally thick neck   ▢ adverb   ▢ adjective   ▢ noun

c You could **post-modify** your chosen **noun** with a **prepositional phrase** (phrase that can add descriptive information to nouns):

a large man with heavy, broad shoulders   ▢ adjective   ▢ noun   ▢ prepositional phrase

a dark grey shadow beneath the skin   ▢ adjectives   ▢ noun   ▢ prepositional phrase

How do different language choices affect description and its impact?

Look at some of the sentences from the *Scorpia Rising* extract again – but now with all the adjectives and prepositional phrases removed.

Zeljan Kurst was a .... man .... He was bald .... His head had been shaved and there was a .... shadow .... His eyes .... showed intelligence and he had the .... lips and .... nose of a wrestler, or perhaps a bouncer at a .... nightclub.

Compare the sentences above with the extract on page 16. How have these changes affected the impact of the description on the reader?

Activity 2

Look at the story you planned in Activity 5 on page 5. What kind of villain will yours be? What would you like your description of this villain to suggest?

1   a   Write down three to five words or phrases that sum up the impression you want your villain to make on your reader.

    b   Note down some descriptive details you could use to create this impression. You could write your ideas down in a table like the one below.

I want the reader to think my villain is	A detail I could use to suggest this could be
ruthless and cruel	blue eyes – cold, emotionless, staring
involved in violence	scar on face

> ### What do better writers do?
>
> Better writers expand nouns with expanded noun phrases with **adjectives**, **adverbs** and **prepositional phrases** to make their descriptions of characters and settings more vivid for the reader.

2   a   Write two or three sentences describing your villain, using only **unexpanded** nouns.

    b   Add some **adjectives** to pre- or post-modify each of your nouns.

    c   Add some **adverbs** to pre-modify one or two of your adjectives.

    d   Add some **prepositional phrases** to post-modify one or two of your nouns.

    e   Which of your choices are effective? Which are not? Decide which to keep and which to cross out.

CHECK YOUR WRITING

  ➔   Look back at your writing from Activity 2 question 2.

1   a   Does your description effectively suggest the character you imagined in Activity 2 question 1?

    b   Which of your decisions work well in establishing this character? Write a sentence or two explaining how.

    c   How could you add even more vivid detail and variety to your description?

  ⬇   Which column in the table below do you think best describes your writing?

I chose some adjectives and adverbs deliberately to describe a villainous character.	I chose some adjectives, adverbs and prepositional phrases deliberately to create the impression I wanted my reader to have of this villain.	I carefully and deliberately chose a varied range of adjectives, adverbs and prepositional phrases to create the impression I wanted my reader to have of this villain.

Assessment: Spies and villains

Learning objective

- Understand how to write a short story extract using a range of features for effect

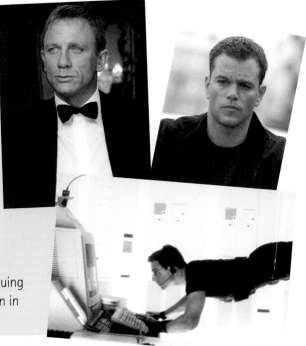

So far in this unit, you have explored:

- the key features of the spy fiction genre
- narrative structure: exposition, conflict, climax and resolution
- writing a story opening to grab your reader's attention
- using paragraphing and verbs to create a sense of pace and threat
- choosing first or third person to establish your narrative viewpoint
- building descriptions of characters using longer noun phrases.

You will use all the skills you have developed so far to craft a short, intriguing and engaging extract from a spy story. Your hero will encounter the villain in a difficult and dangerous situation.

PLAN

Follow the steps below to collect your ideas and make important decisions before you start writing.

REMEMBER your answer to question 1 when you make all other decisions about your writing.

1   What kind of impact do I want my extract to have on the reader?

Excitement?   Danger?   Tension?

Action?   Humour?   A mixture of these?

2   What kind of hero will I have in this story?

Male?   Female?   Old?   Young?   Courageous and strong, or cunning and hugely intelligent?

Loud and arrogant, or quietly confident?   Suave and sophisticated, or rough and ready for anything?

3   What kind of villain will I have in this story?

Male?   Female?   Old?   Young?   Similar to the hero or completely different?

A ruthless psychopath, or a controlling, manipulative genius?   A wealthy megalomaniac or a desperate gangster?

4 Why have the hero and the villain met?

Who is in control of the situation, hero or villain?

Has your hero been caught sneaking into the villain's headquarters?

Has your hero cornered the villain?

Have they met by accident and recognised each other?

5 In what setting will my hero and villain meet?

Will they be alone, or in a crowded place?

Has the villain brought people with him/her?

Does your hero have any back-up?

6 What narrative viewpoint will I use?

First person from the hero's point of view?

First person from the villain's point of view?

Third person, focusing mainly on the hero?

7 What will I include in my extract?

Description of the villain?

Description of the hero's thoughts and feelings?

Description of the setting?

Dialogue between the hero and the villain?

Description of the action?

All of these?

Or just some of these?

WRITE

You are now ready to write your extract. Keep your plan in front of you as you write, to remind you of the decisions you have made and why.

Your mission:

Write a short extract from a spy story in which the hero meets the villain in a difficult or dangerous situation.

Aim to write between 150 and 200 words.

REFLECT

1   When you have completed your extract, read it through carefully.

   a   Are you pleased with it? Which of the following do you feel you have achieved?

☐ I think I have chosen the most effective narrative viewpoint for this story extract
☐ I think I grab the reader's attention from the start
☐ I think I describe the setting effectively
☐ I think I describe my characters effectively
☐ I think my choice of verbs creates a sense of drama and threat
☐ I think my paragraphing gives my writing pace and drama
☐ I think my writing will have the impact I want it to have on the reader

   b   For each of the statements you feel you have achieved, write a sentence explaining the effect and impact of your choices. For example:

My use of a first person narrator meant that I could really focus the reader's attention on what my hero was thinking and feeling.

2   a   Look back at the list in question 1a. Choose one or two areas that you feel you could improve.

   b   Working on your own or with a partner, look back at the relevant pages in this unit to remind yourself of the choices and techniques you could use to improve your writing in those one or two areas.

   c   Write a sentence or two explaining how you will improve your writing in those one or two areas. For example:

I can increase the sense of action and danger in my writing by choosing more descriptive verbs such as 'leap' instead of 'jump'.

   d   Now make the improvements you want to make to your writing and compare it with your old version. Has it improved? You could ask your partner to give you their opinion.

6 Building description

Learning objective

- Understand how to develop simple sentences in order to add interesting and vivid detail to a narrative

A **JAMES BOND** NOVEL

DEVIL MAY CARE
Sebastian Faulks
WRITING AS IAN FLEMING

Simple sentences are not just short sentences consisting of a few basic words. They can be crafted to include lots of interesting detail and description.

Activity 1

Read the extract below. It is from Sebastian Faulks' novel, *Devil May Care*.

Hashim works for an undercover organisation. He is waiting to meet a contact...

He stepped out into the rain, looking rapidly back and forth beneath the sodium light. His face was a greyish brown, pocked and wary, with a large, curved nose jutting out between black brows. He tapped the back pocket of his blue ***ouvrier's*** trousers, where, wrapped in a polythene bag, he carried twenty-five thousand new francs. It was the largest amount he had ever had to deal with, and even a man of his experience was right to be apprehensive.

Ducking into the shadows, he glanced down for the fifth or sixth time at his watch. He never knew who he was looking out for because it was never the same man twice. That was part of the excellence of the scheme: the cut-out at each end, the endless supply of new runners. Hashim tried to keep it equally secure when he shipped the goods on. He insisted on different locations and asked for fresh contacts, but it wasn't always possible. Precautions cost money, and although Hashim's buyers were desperate, they knew the street value of what they dealt in. No one in the chain made enough money to be able to act in absolute safety: no one, that is, except some ultimate, all-powerful controller thousands of miles away from the stench of the stairwell where Hashim was now standing.

> **Glossary**
> ***ouvrier:*** worker, labourer

Sticking a soft blue pack of Gauloises to his mouth, he wrapped his lips round a single cigarette and drew it out. As he fired his cheap disposable lighter, a voice spoke in the darkness. Hashim leaped back into the shadow, angry with himself that he'd allowed someone to observe him. His hand went to the side pocket of his trousers, where it felt the outline of the knife that had been his constant companion since his childhood in the slums of Algiers.

A short figure in an army greatcoat came into the sodium light. The hat he wore looked like an old kepi of the Foreign Legion, and water ran from its peak. Hashim couldn't see the face. The man spoke in English, softly, in a rasping voice. 'In Flanders fields,' he said, 'the poppies blow.' Hashim repeated the syllables he had learned by sound alone, with no idea of what they meant: 'Betveen de crosses, row on row.'

The runner laid down a brown, canvas bag on the bottom of the steps and stood back. He had both hands in the pocket of his coat, and Hashim had no doubt that one would be clasping a gun.

1 Choose one word, phrase or sentence that gives you a strong impression of the character of Hashim. What impression does your chosen word, phrase or sentence give you? Write a sentence or two explaining your ideas.

2 Choose one word, phrase or sentence which gives you a strong impression of the other character in the extract: the man Hashim meets. What impression does your chosen word, phrase or sentence give you? Write a sentence or two explaining your ideas.

WRITER'S WORKSHOP: Simple sentences

How can I develop simple sentences to add detail and description?

Simple sentences consist of one main clause giving the reader
one key piece of information. They contain one **verb**:

A man came.   ■ noun   ■ verb

Writers can use lots of different ways to add detail and description to a simple sentence.

- They can choose interesting, descriptive **nouns**:

A figure came.   ■ noun   ■ verb

- They can add **adjectives** and **prepositional phrases** to expand the **noun phrase**
and tell the reader what something or someone is like:

A short figure in an army greatcoat came.   *expanded noun phrase*

☐ adjective   ■ noun   ☐ prepositional phrase   ■ verb

- They can add **adverbs** and **adverbials** to tell the reader when, where or how something happens:

A short figure in an army greatcoat came into the sodium light.

☐ adjective   ■ noun   ☐ prepositional phrase   ■ verb   ■ adverbial phrase (of place)

What impression has the writer given you in this sentence of the man who suddenly appears? How has the writer's choice of noun, adjective, prepositional phrase and adverbial created this impression?

Look again at all the different versions of the sentence above. Which version do you prefer? Write a sentence or two explaining your choice.

Activity 2

1   Look again at the sentence from the extract:

> A short figure in an army greatcoat came into the sodium light.

Try changing the writer's choices:

a   Think of a **noun** to replace 'figure'.

b   Think of a **verb** to replace 'came'.

c   Think of an **adjective** to replace 'short'.

d   Think of a **prepositional phrase** to replace 'in an army greatcoat'.

e   Think of an **adverb** or **adverbial phrase** to replace 'into the sodium light'.

f   Better writers do not overload their sentences with description. What is the effect of each of the changes you have made? Which of your choices add to the reader's impression of this character? Which do not? Decide which to keep and which to cross out.

2   Writers structure their sentences for impact and emphasis. For example, compare the original sentence from the extract (shown above) with this version:

> Into the sodium light, in an army greatcoat, came a short figure.

a   How has the new version changed the emphasis and effect of the sentence? Has it made it more or less dramatic and tense?

b   Try reorganising the version of the sentence you decided on in question 1f above. How many different ways can you structure it? What different effects can you create?

Activity 3

1   Look again at the extract on pages 22 and 23.

a   What do you think will happen next?

b   Write the next paragraph of the story. Aim to write at least three simple sentences, using carefully chosen nouns and verbs and developing them with adjectives, adverbs, adverbial phrases or prepositional phrases. Always think about the effect your choices will have on the reader.

Look again at the extract on pages 22 and 23.

What do better writers do?

Better writers often use simple sentences, constructed with carefully selected detail and language choices, but do not overload their sentences with description.

CHECK YOUR WRITING

➡ Look back at your writing from Activity 3 above. Annotate your writing, explaining your choices and the effect they created.

⬇ Which column in the table below do you think best describes your writing?

I used some adjectives and adverbs to develop my simple sentences.	I used a variety of adjectives, adverbial phrases and prepositional phrases to develop my simple sentences, some of which I chose for effect.	I used a variety of adjectives, adverbial phrases and prepositional phrases to develop my simple sentences, all carefully chosen to achieve the effect I wanted to create.

7 Building sentences

Learning objective

- Understand how to use conjunctions and clauses to make your meaning clear

You can create more variety in the structure of your sentences by linking them with joining words, or **conjunctions**.

Activity 1

Look at this paragraph from the *Devil May Care* extract on page 23:

> Sticking a soft blue pack of Gauloises to his mouth, he wrapped his lips round a single cigarette and drew it out. As he fired his cheap disposable lighter, a voice spoke in the darkness. Hashim leaped back into the shadow, angry with himself that he'd allowed someone to observe him.

Now look at the same passage, rewritten using only simple sentences:

> He stuck a soft blue pack of Gauloises to his mouth. He wrapped his lips round a single cigarette. He drew it out. He fired his cheap disposable lighter. A voice spoke in the darkness. Hashim leaped back into the shadow. He was angry with himself. He'd allowed someone to observe him.

Try reading both versions aloud.

a Which one **sounds better**?

b Which one makes **clearer sense**?

c Which one is more **interesting** to read?

d Which version do you prefer – the original version or the rewritten version? Write a sentence or two explaining your choice.

WRITER'S WORKSHOP: Varying sentence structure

How can I use coordinating conjunctions and coordinate clauses to make my meaning clear?

Look at this sentence from the extract on page 22:

> He insisted on different locations and asked for fresh contacts, but it wasn't always possible.

The writer could have written this using three **simple sentences**.

> He insisted on different locations. He asked for fresh contacts. It wasn't always possible.

Instead the writer decided to link these three clauses together using the **coordinating conjunctions** 'and' and 'but':

> He insisted on different locations ⟨and⟩ asked for fresh contacts, ⟨but⟩ it wasn't always possible.

▮ coordinate clause 1   ▮ coordinate clause 2   ▮ coordinate clause 3

Compare the version containing three simple sentences with the version using coordinating conjunctions. How do the coordinating conjunctions help the reader to understand the writer's meaning?

> Coordinating conjunctions include:
> and   but   or   so

How can I use subordinating conjunctions and subordinate clauses to make my meaning clear?

Now look at this sentence from the extract on page 23:

> As he fired his cheap disposable lighter, a voice spoke in the darkness.

The writer could have written this using two simple sentences.

> *He fired his cheap disposable lighter. A voice spoke in the darkness.*

Instead the writer decided to link these two clauses using the subordinating conjunction 'as'.

> As he fired his cheap disposable lighter, a voice spoke in the darkness.

▇ subordinate clause

▇ main clause

Compare the version containing two simple sentences with the version using a subordinating conjunction. How does the subordinating conjunction help the reader to understand the writer's meaning?

Subordinating conjunctions include:

although	as	when
whenever	if	because
unless	while	until
whereas		

Activity 2

1 Look again at the extract you explored in Activity 1. What happens if you swap the clauses in each sentence?

For example, if you swap these two clauses...

> As he fired his cheap disposable lighter, a voice spoke in the darkness.

...you get this sentence:

> A voice spoke in the darkness as he fired his cheap disposable lighter.

a Does it still make sense?

b Does it have the same meaning?

c Does it have the same impact?

2 Look again at the writing you completed in Activity 3 on page 25.

a Continue the story, writing another paragraph using a range of simple sentences as well as some coordinate clauses and some subordinate clauses introduced by conjunctions.

b Annotate your writing, explaining why you have made these choices.

What do better writers do?

Better writers use coordinating and subordinating conjunctions to link their ideas and make their meaning clear to the reader.

Learning objective

- Understand how sentences can be structured to create emphasis, pace, tension and drama

Successful writers not only use a range of sentence structures to make their meaning clear; they also think about how their sentences are structured to create emphasis, pace, tension and drama.

Activity 1

In Activity 2 on page 27 you experimented with the structure of a sentence by swapping the **main clause** and the **subordinate clause** around.

Swapping the sentence's two clauses did not destroy the sense or change the meaning of the sentence – but it did change the **emphasis** of the sentence.

Look at some more sentences from the extract on pages 22–23.

1 For each one, try restructuring the sentence in two or three different ways by re-ordering the clauses and phrases.

2 Write a sentence or two explaining what each version is emphasising, or any other difference the restructuring has made.

a   As he fired his cheap disposable lighter

a voice spoke in the darkness.

b   Ducking into the shadows

he glanced down   for the fifth or sixth time

at his watch.

c   He tapped the back pocket of his blue *ouvrier*'s trousers

wrapped in a polythene bag

where

he carried twenty-five thousand new francs.

Activity 2

Read the text below. It is another extract from *Devil May Care* by Sebastian Faulks, following on from the extract you read on pages 22–23.

Hashim has met his contact and is handing over a large amount of money in exchange for a package.

The runner laid down a brown, canvas bag on the bottom of the steps and stood back. He had both hands in the pocket of his coat, and Hashim had no doubt that one would be clasping a gun. From the back pocket of his blue trousers, Hashim took out the polythene-wrapped money, then stepped back. This was how it was always done: no touching, and a safe distance maintained. The man bent down and took the money. He didn't pause to count it, merely inclined his head as he stowed the package inside his coat. Then he in turn stood back and waited for Hashim to move.

Hashim bent down to the step and lifted the bag. The weight felt good, heavier than he had known before, but not so heavy as to make him suspect it was bulked out with sand. The business was concluded and he waited for the other man to move off.

Reluctant to move first, Hashim faced the other man. He suddenly became aware of the noise around him – the roar of the traffic, the sound of rain dripping from the walkway on to the ground.

Something wasn't right. Hashim began to move along the wall, furtive, like a lizard, edging towards the freedom of the night. In two strides the man was on him, his arm across Hashim's throat. Then the unpainted wall smashed into his face, flattening the curved nose into a formless pulp. Hashim felt himself thrown face down on the concrete floor, and heard the click of a safety catch being released as a gun barrel pressed behind his ear. With his free hand, and with practised dexterity, the man pulled Hashim's arms behind his back and handcuffed them together.

1   Many of the sentences in the extract use the coordinating conjunction 'and' to link coordinate clauses. What effect does this have on the reader?

2   How else has the writer used different types of clause and different sentence lengths to create pace, tension and drama in this extract?

   a   Choose **three** sentences that you think have been written for effect.

   b   For each one, write a sentence or two exploring the impact, emphasis or effect the writer wanted to achieve.

29

WRITER'S WORKSHOP: Structuring sentences for effect

How can I structure my sentences to create different effects?

Short sentences can be used to create tension or a moment of dramatic impact.

Something wasn't right.

Coordinate clauses can convey lots of information or a series of events.

The runner laid down a brown, canvas bag on the bottom of the steps and stood back.

Using the coordinating conjunction 'and' conveys a sense of pace, of events moving quickly, adding tension to the scene.

Subordinate clauses can add detail or give information about two events happening at the same time.

Then the unpainted wall smashed into his face, flattening the curved nose into a formless pulp.

Subordinate clauses can be positioned to delay dramatic moments in your story, giving more emphasis and impact.

Hashim began to move along the wall, furtive, like a lizard, edging towards the freedom of the night.

The writer delays and emphasises the drama and tension of Hashim 'edging towards the freedom of the night' by positioning it at the end of the sentence.

What do better writers do?

Better writers craft their sentences carefully. They think about the length and structure of their sentences, and the impact each one will have on the reader, whether it's to convey information, to emphasise a particular point, or to increase the pace, tension or drama of their story.

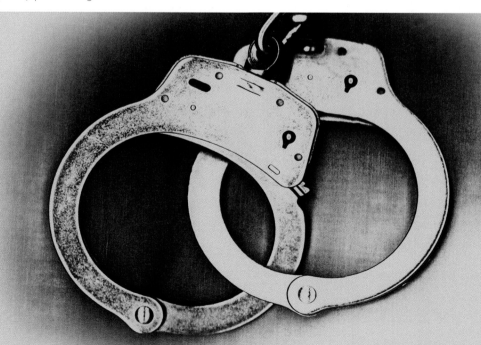

Activity 3

1 You are going to write a short extract from a spy story.
In the extract, like Hashim in the *Devil May Care* extract,
your hero is waiting to meet someone.
Who might they be meeting?

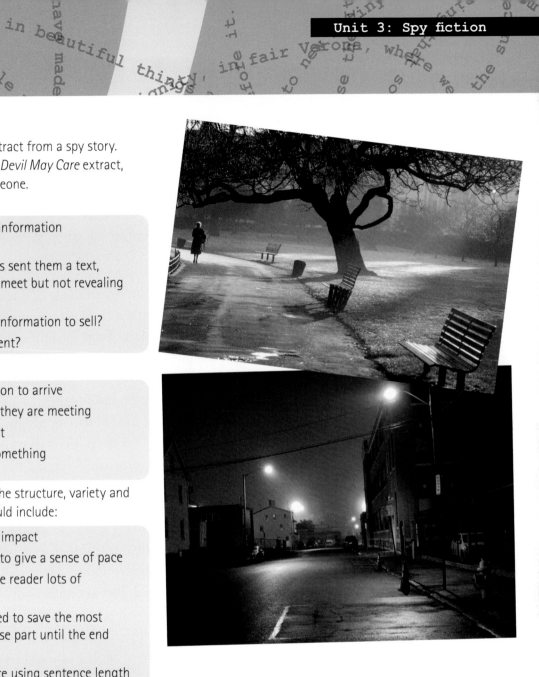

- Another spy to find out what information
they have discovered?
- A mysterious stranger who has sent them a text,
naming the time and place to meet but not revealing
their name?
- Someone who has top secret information to sell?
- Or someone completely different?

You could describe:

- your hero waiting for the person to arrive
- the appearance of the person they are meeting
- what happens when they meet
- all or some of the above, or something
completely different.

2 Write your extract, focusing on the structure, variety and
effect of your sentences. You could include:

- a short sentence for dramatic impact
- a series of coordinate clauses to give a sense of pace
- subordinate clauses to give the reader lots of
descriptive detail
- a subordinate clause positioned to save the most
important, or dramatic, or tense part until the end
of the sentence
- any other effect you can create using sentence length
or structure.

CHECK YOUR WRITING

➡ Look back at your writing from Activity 3. Annotate your writing to explain some of the decisions you made about
sentence length and structure, and the effect they created.

⬇ Which column in the table below do you think best describes your writing?

I used a variety of simple sentences, coordinate and subordinate clauses and coordinating and subordinating conjunctions.	I used a variety of simple sentences, coordinate and subordinate clauses and coordinating and subordinating conjunctions, some of which I chose for effect.	I used a variety of simple sentences, coordinate and subordinate clauses and coordinating and subordinating conjunctions, choosing and structuring them carefully to achieve the effect I wanted to create.

31

Learning objectives

- Understand what is meant by a minor sentence
- Understand how to use minor sentences for effect

You have explored how to use a range of sentence structures to achieve different effects in your writing. Another way you can do this is by breaking the rules of formal standard English grammar: by using short fragments of sentences for effect.

Activity 1

Read the extract below. It is from *The Hidden Man* by Charles Cumming.

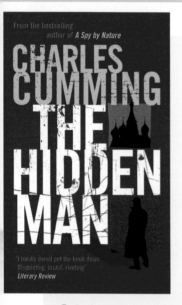

The Russian is sitting alone on the driver's side of a rented Mercedes Benz. The key in the ignition has been turned a single click, just enough to power the radio, and it is snowing outside, wet flakes of soft ice falling like ash in the darkness. A song comes on, an old Sinatra tune the man has not heard in many years: Frank singing live to a room full of screaming Americans, hanging off his every note. Sometimes it feels as if his whole life has been lived inside parked cars listening to the radio: sudden movements on side streets; a light snuffing out in a bedroom four floors up; moments of snatched sleep. Cars that smelled of imported cigarettes and the sweat of tired, unwashed men.

A young couple turn the corner into the street ahead of him, walking arm in arm with a jaunty, light-hearted step. Drunk, most probably, coming towards the car and laughing up at the falling snow. They are delighted by it, letting the flakes melt in the palms of upturned hands, embracing one another as it settles in their hair and on their clothes. Like so many London girls, he thinks the woman is worryingly thin: legs like saplings in high-heeled shoes. He fears that she may topple over on the wet pavement and, if she hurts herself, he will have to get out of the car to help her. Then there will be two witnesses who have seen his face.

The song ends and fades into an advertisement narrated in slang and dialect, words he cannot make out. English is no longer clear to him; somehow, in recent years, the language has changed, it has moved away. The couple skip past the Mercedes and he watches them disappear down the street using the mirror on the passenger side. An old technique. No need even to turn his head.

Now he reaches down to switch off the radio and everything is once again silent. Just a very faint impression of traffic in the distance, the city's constant hum. Then, as an extension of the same movement, the Russian turns the catch on the glove box with his left hand, holds it as the casing falls open, and takes out the gun.

1   The extract is written in the present tense: 'The Russian is sitting...', not 'The Russian was sitting...' What effect do you think this has?

2   Look at this definition of a sentence:

> **Sentence** (*noun*): A group of words that expresses a statement, question, command etc, and contains at least one verb. Sentences start with a capital letter and end with either a full stop, a question mark or an exclamation mark.

Can you identify any sentences in the extract that do not fit this definition?

WRITER'S WORKSHOP: Using minor sentences

How can I use minor sentences to give a sense of pace and urgency?

Minor sentences are a type of sentence that does not contain a main verb. They may contain no verb at all, or they may contain a **non-finite verb**.

A **non-finite verb** may be:

- a **present participle** ending in '-ing', such as 'sleeping' or 'running'
- a **past participle** ending in '-ed', such as 'killed' or 'watched' (there are, however, irregular past participles such as 'slept' or 'ran')
- an **infinitive**, the basic form of a verb, which begins with 'to', such as 'to be' or 'to spy'.

Look at these examples of minor sentences from the extract on page 32:

Drunk, most probably, coming towards the car and laughing up at the falling snow.

non-finite verb (present participle)

An old technique. ← no verb

No need even to turn his head.

non-finite verb (infinitive)

Minor sentences are not often used in formal written standard English. However, they are regularly used in spoken English and frequently used in fiction. Writers use them to:

- give their writing a feel of spoken English – as though the writer is talking directly to the reader
- give their writing a sense of pace and urgency – as though the narrator is hurrying to get their story onto the page.

Activity 2

1 You are going to write a short extract from a spy story in which your hero is waiting and watching for someone – just like the Russian in the extract from *The Hidden Man*.

Before you start writing, note down some ideas:

- **Where** are they waiting?
- What do they **see** as they wait?
- How do they **feel** as they wait?
- What kind of **mood** or **atmosphere** do you want to create in your extract?
- What **techniques** will you use to give your writing tension and pace?

2 Write your extract. Aim to write around 100 words using:

- the present tense
- some minor sentences, thinking about the effect you want each one to create.

What do better writers do?

Better writers do not overload their writing with minor sentences. They add them to the variety of simple, compound and complex sentences to give their writing pace and energy.

10 Effective starters

- Understand how to start sentences
  in a range of ways to create
  variety, pace, drama or emphasis
  in your writing

The way you structure your sentences – particularly the first word or two – can influence the way your reader will respond to your ideas.

Activity 1

1   Look at the extracts below. They are taken from the opening four sentences of *The Hidden Man* extract that you read on page 32.

A

The Russian is sitting alone on the driver's side of a rented Mercedes Benz. The key in the ignition has been turned a single click, just enough to power the radio.

B

A song comes on, an old Sinatra tune the man has not heard in many years.

C

Sometimes it feels as if his whole life has been lived inside parked cars listening to the radio.

Now look at these sentences. They tell the same story – but they have been rewritten.

A   He is sitting alone on the driver's side of a rented Mercedes Benz. He has turned the key in the ignition a single click, just enough to power the radio.

B   He hears a song come on, an old Sinatra tune he has not heard in many years.

C   He feels sometimes as if his whole life has been lived inside parked cars listening to the radio.

a   What is the key difference between the two versions?

b   How does this difference change the effect the opening might have on the reader? Write a sentence or two explaining your ideas.

2   Look again at the extract from *The Hidden Man* on page 32. Make a note of the first word of each sentence in a table like the one below. Each time the writer repeats the word at the start of a sentence, add a mark to your tally. For example, the first two sentences start with the word 'The'. The third sentence starts with the word 'A'.

Word	Number of times used
The	II
A	I

3   The extract contains 19 sentences. Look back at some of the writing you have completed in this unit. Make a table like the one above, recording the first words of 19 of your sentences.

4   Compare the tally of first words from the extract with the tally from your own writing. What do you notice? Who has achieved the greatest variety in their sentence starters?

WRITER'S WORKSHOP: Achieving sentence variety

How can I achieve more sentence variety in my writing?

There are lots of ways to start a sentence:

- A **determiner**,
  e.g. a, an, the, my, your, his, her, our, their

  > The Russian is sitting alone on the driver's side of a rented Mercedes Benz.

- A **pronoun**, e.g. I, you, he, she, it, we, they

  > They are delighted by it

- An **adverb** or **adverbial phrase**:
  * an adverb or adverbial phrase of manner (how?) e.g. quickly
  * an adverb or adverbial phrase of time (when?) e.g. occasionally, every evening, that night
  * an adverb or adverbial phrase of place (where?) e.g. beneath the floorboards, above his head

  > Sometimes it feels as if his whole life has been lived inside parked cars

- A **non-finite verb**, e.g. running, crawling, cracked

  > Ducking into the shadows, he glanced down for the fifth or sixth time at his watch.

- An **adjective**, e.g. slow, huge, violent

  > Drunk, most probably

- A **subordinating** or **coordinating conjunction**,
  e.g. if, although, as, but, and

  > As he fired his cheap disposable lighter, a voice spoke in the darkness.

What do better writers do?

Better writers think about the ways in which they start their sentences. They use a variety of vocabulary and a number of different grammatical ways to start their sentences. This can give the writing pace, rhythm or emphasis, making it more engaging for readers.

Activity 2

1 Look again at the opening sentence from *The Hidden Man*:

> The Russian is sitting alone on the driver's side of a rented Mercedes Benz.

a In how many different ways can you restructure or rewrite the opening sentence? Try starting each different version with a different word or grammatical feature from the list on page 35. For example:

> He *is sitting alone on the driver's side of a rented Mercedes Benz.*

▢ pronoun

or

> Fidgeting uncomfortably, *the Russian is sitting alone on the driver's side of a rented Mercedes Benz.*

▢ non-finite verb ▢ adverb

b For each different version you have written of the opening sentence, write a sentence or two commenting on the effect you think your changes have had.

Activity 3

1 Look back at the writing you completed in Activity 2 on page 33. Write the next paragraph of your story. Your hero could still be watching and waiting for someone – or perhaps they see someone or something suspicious. Aim to write around 100 words, thinking about the way you start your sentences.

2 Make a tally of the first word or phrase in each of your sentences, and the type of word you have used. You could record your tally in a table like the one below:

Word/phrase	Word type	Tally
The	Determiner	II
Five minutes earlier	Adverbial phrase of time	I
Looking	Non-finite verb	I

CHECK YOUR WRITING

→ Look back at your writing from Activity 2 on page 33.

1   Have you used the present tense consistently in your writing? Check to make sure and correct any errors. For example:.

> *edges*
> He ~~edged~~ towards the front door and sees a silhouette through the glass.

2   Annotate your writing, highlighting one or two examples of the present tense. What is the effect of using the present tense (e.g. 'he leaps over the wall') rather than the past tense (e.g. 'he leapt over the wall')?

3   Annotate your writing to highlight any minor sentences you have used. Identify whether they:

- contain no verb, for example:

> *Silent.*   *Perfectly still.*

- contain a non-finite verb: a present participle, a past participle, or an infinitive. For example:

> *Waiting for the knock at the door.*   ▨ present participle

4   Choose two of your minor sentences. Add to your annotation, writing a sentence or two about the effect you wanted each one to have. It might look something like this:

> Present tense makes the reader feel like he is living through the experience with the character and watching as it happens.
>
> *He edges towards the front door and sees a silhouette through the glass.*
> *He waits. Silent. Perfectly still. Waiting for the knock at the door.*
>
> Minor sentences with no verbs add impact and sound hurried and anxious, creating a jumpy, tense atmosphere.
>
> This minor sentence with present participle builds a tense atmosphere, emphasising the length of time he is 'waiting'.

↓ Look back at your writing from Activity 3 above. Which column in the table below do you think best describes your writing?

I have used a range of sentence lengths and structures. I have tried to start my sentences in lots of different ways.	I have used a range of sentence lengths and structures. I have tried to structure some of them for variety, pace, drama or emphasis.	I have used a range of sentence lengths and structures, intentionally structuring them to create a range of effects, including variety, pace, drama and emphasis.

11 Spy speak

Learning objective

- Understand how dialogue can be punctuated and structured using identifiers to imitate the patterns and rhythm of real, natural speech

Dialogue is a key feature of most fiction. What a character says – and how they say it – can not only help to tell the story, but also reveal a great deal about the character.

Activity 1

Read the extract below. It is from *Restless* by William Boyd.

Eva's brother has been killed. His boss, Romer, has come to talk to Eva and tell her that her brother was a spy.

WILLIAM BOYD
RESTLESS

NOW A MAJOR BBC DRAMA

BESTSELLING AUTHOR OF ANY HUMAN HEART AND WAITING FOR SUNRISE
BLOOMSBURY

'Kolia was working for me when he was killed,' Romer said.

'You told me.'

'He was killed by Fascists, by Nazis.'

'I thought he was robbed.'

'He was doing…' he paused. 'He was doing dangerous work – and he was discovered. I think he was betrayed.'

Eva wanted to speak but decided to say nothing. Now, in the silence, Romer removed his cigarette case again and went through the rigmarole of putting the cigarette in his mouth, patting his pockets for his lighter, removing the cigarette from his mouth, tapping both ends on the cigarette case, pulling the ashtray on her father's desk towards him, lighting the cigarette and inhaling and exhaling strongly. Eva watched all this, trying to stay completely impassive.

'I work for the British government,' he said. 'You understand what I mean…'

'Yes,' Eva said, 'I think so.'

Look closely at the dialogue in the extract.

1. At the end of the first line, the writer uses an **identifier** ('Romer said' identifies who is speaking):

    > 'Kolia was working for me when he was killed,' Romer said.

    In the next three lines, the writer lets the reader work out for themselves who is speaking.

    > 'You told me.'
    >
    > 'He was killed by Fascists, by Nazis.'
    >
    > 'I thought he was robbed.'

    Why do you think the writer has done this?

2. In the final two lines, the writer interrupts each character's dialogue with an identifier:

    > 'I work for the British government,' he said.
    > 'You understand what I mean…'
    > 'Yes,' Eva said, 'I think so.'

    a. Experiment with rewriting these last two lines. You could:

    - remove 'he said' and 'Eva said' altogether
    - reposition 'he said' and 'Eva said' at the end of, or at a different point in the dialogue.

    b. Which version do you prefer?

    c. What effect does removing or repositioning 'he said' and 'Eva said' have?

    d. Why do you think the writer chose to position these identifiers as he did?

WRITER'S WORKSHOP: Punctuating dialogue

How should I punctuate dialogue?

These are two of the key rules you need to follow when you punctuate speech in your story:

- Use speech marks to show which words are spoken by a character.
- Put a punctuation mark at the end of every piece of dialogue before the speech marks.

For example:

> 'Kolia was working for me when he was killed,' Romer said.
> 'You told me.'

▇ speech marks show what is said

▇ capital letter at the start of speech

▇ comma before closing speech marks because followed by identifier

▇ full stop before closing speech marks because not followed by identifier

How can I punctuate dialogue to make it realistic?

Real people do not always speak in full sentences. Sometimes they pause to think. Sometimes they stop speaking in the middle of sentences. You can recreate this with punctuation in your characters' dialogue to make it sound more like real speech – and to add drama and tension.

- You can use **dashes** – like these – to suggest a pause in the middle of a sentence.

  You can also use **dashes** to suggest someone has been interrupted or stopped speaking abruptly.

- You can use an **ellipsis** (three dots) ... to suggest that someone has stopped speaking or left a dramatic pause.

Activity 2

1 Look at this example of dialogue from the extract on page 38:

> 'He was doing…' he paused. 'He was doing dangerous work – and he was discovered. I think he was betrayed.'

Here the writer has used an **ellipsis** and a **dash**. What different effects has the writer created by using these two different punctuation marks?

2 **a** Imagine a conversation between a spy and their boss. What might they be discussing? It could be:

- a new mission
- a recently completed mission
- the spy's future – will they continue to work for the organisation?

b Write the dialogue between the spy and their boss. Think carefully about:

- using accurate speech punctuation
- using ellipses and dashes for effect
- omitting or placing identifiers for effect.

What do better writers do?

Better writers use a range of punctuation in their dialogue. They use speech punctuation accurately and use identifiers and punctuation such as dashes and ellipses to imitate the patterns and rhythm of real, natural speech.

12 Planning a complete spy story

Learning objective

- Understand how to plan a short story

Your final mission in this unit will be to write a short spy story. Before you can start writing, you need to gather your ideas. You might want to re-use some of the ideas you came up with earlier in the unit – or you might want to start from scratch. Use the activities below to plan your story.

Activity 1

1 Before you think about what will happen in your story, think about the ingredients you definitely want to include in it: characters, events, settings or anything else. Have another look at the list of spy story ingredients on page 3 to help you. Make a list of the ones you definitely want to include in your story.

2 Now you need the basic idea for your story. But where do story ideas come from?

You could start with a **setting**. You might want to set your story in one or more of these places:

Or you could start with a **single incident** and see what ideas develop. It might be something like one of these:

3 Now you need to structure your story, using the four-part narrative structure:

| Exposition | Conflict | Climax | Resolution |

Look back at the work you did on page 4 if you need a reminder of this structure.

Decide what will happen in each of the four stages of your story. You could use some of the ideas below, or come up with your own.

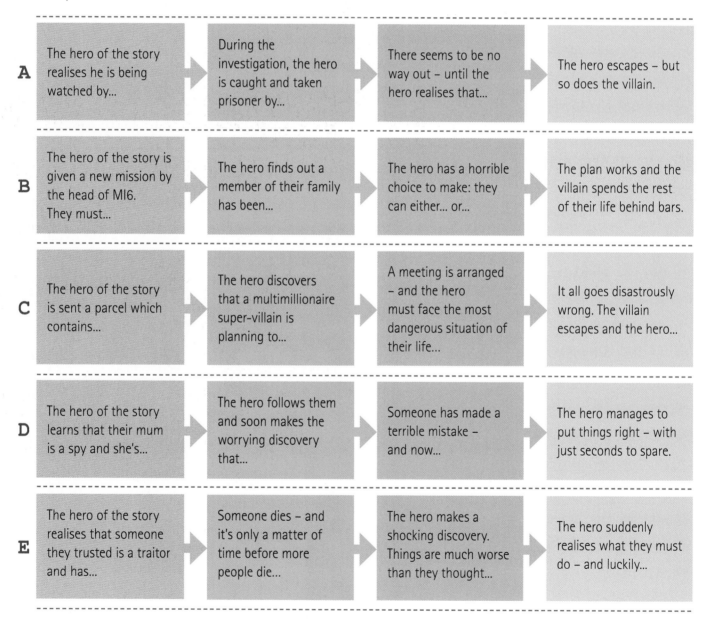

A
- The hero of the story realises he is being watched by...
- During the investigation, the hero is caught and taken prisoner by...
- There seems to be no way out – until the hero realises that...
- The hero escapes – but so does the villain.

B
- The hero of the story is given a new mission by the head of MI6. They must...
- The hero finds out a member of their family has been...
- The hero has a horrible choice to make: they can either... or...
- The plan works and the villain spends the rest of their life behind bars.

C
- The hero of the story is sent a parcel which contains...
- The hero discovers that a multimillionaire super-villain is planning to...
- A meeting is arranged – and the hero must face the most dangerous situation of their life...
- It all goes disastrously wrong. The villain escapes and the hero...

D
- The hero of the story learns that their mum is a spy and she's...
- The hero follows them and soon makes the worrying discovery that...
- Someone has made a terrible mistake – and now...
- The hero manages to put things right – with just seconds to spare.

E
- The hero of the story realises that someone they trusted is a traitor and has...
- Someone dies – and it's only a matter of time before more people die...
- The hero makes a shocking discovery. Things are much worse than they thought...
- The hero suddenly realises what they must do – and luckily...

Activity 2

You now need to think about some of the decisions you will have to make before you start writing. Answer the questions below to help you.

1 What kind of impact do I want my story to have on the reader?

Write a sentence or two explaining your decision.

2 What narrative viewpoint will I use?

Write a sentence or two explaining your choice.

3 What kinds of nouns and verbs will I use?

These will help you to describe characters and settings and to create tension. Think about the characters, settings and situations you have planned and add a word bank of relevant nouns and verbs to your planning.

4 What about descriptive details?

Again, think about the settings and situations and characters you have planned and add a bank of relevant descriptive details to your planning. You might think of adjectives, adverbs or prepositional phrases.

5 Could I experiment with different sentence structures?

Add some reminders to your plan. Some examples might be simple sentences or coordinate clauses.

What do better writers do?

Better writers:

- use the key features of their chosen genre, but try to make their stories original and not copy ideas from other books or films

- plan their stories, thinking about the effect they want each stage of their story to have on the reader

- keep their readers guessing. The reader might think the hero will defeat the villain but better writers encourage them to wonder how the hero will achieve this.

CHECK YOUR PLANNING

➡ Look at all the planning for your story. Will the story you have planned:

- use some of the key features of the spy genre?
- grab and hold the reader's attention?
- have a powerful and satisfying ending?
- be clear so that the reader understands exactly what is happening and why?

➡ If you answered 'Maybe', 'I hope so' or 'No' to any of these questions, have another think about your plan and what you can do to improve it.

Assessment: The full story

Learning objective

- Understand how to write a complete short story using the key features of a particular genre

WRITE

You are now ready to complete the final task in this unit:

Your mission:

Write a short story in the spy genre.
Aim to write between 500 and 750 words.

Remember to:

- follow the plan you prepared on pages 40–43
- use all the skills and knowledge you have gained and practised in this unit
- think about the decisions you need to make as a writer
- engage, entertain and thrill your reader.

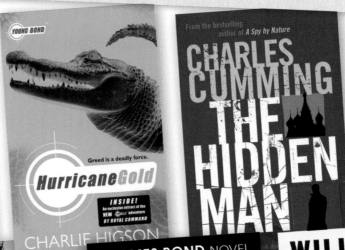

REFLECT

1 When you have finished writing the first draft of your story, read it through carefully.
Are you pleased with it?

  a Which of the following do you feel you have achieved?

☐ I think I have chosen the most effective narrative viewpoint for this story extract

☐ I think I grab the reader's attention from the start

☐ I think I describe the setting effectively

☐ I think I describe my characters effectively

☐ I think my choice of verbs creates a sense of pace and threat

☐ I think my paragraphing gives my writing pace and drama

☐ I think I have used a range of sentence lengths and structures for effect

☐ I think my writing will have the impact I want it to have on the reader

  b For each of the statements you feel you have achieved, write a sentence explaining the effect and impact of your choices.

2 a Choose one or two areas of your writing that you feel you could improve. This might be:

    • making more use of a particular technique in your writing, such as:

Experimenting further with use of paragraphs throughout my story

    or:

    • improving a particular section of your story, such as:

Making the chase through the tunnel more tense and dramatic by using some minor sentences and some short sentences, and choosing more powerful nouns and verbs

  b Working on your own or with a partner, look back at the relevant pages in this unit to remind yourself of the choices and techniques you would use to improve your writing in those one or two areas.

  c Write a sentence or two explaining how you will improve your writing in those one or two areas.

  d Make the improvements you want to make to your writing.

CHECK YOUR WRITING

➡ Put on your teacher's hat and mark your own work. Using a different colour pen (if your story is handwritten) or the comments feature (if your story is word-processed), annotate and explain some of your successes.

It might look something like this:

> Really engaging opening, making reader ask who is he? And why is she watching him? Short/minor sentences make it really dramatic.

She had only been there ten minutes when she saw him. He looked like anyone else. Dark hair, jeans, trainers. She pulled her hat down over her eyes and watched him. Watched him like a hawk.

> Choice of powerful nouns and verbs give sense of danger and fear.
>
> Short paragraphs create pace and tension.

She could hear the (thumping) of her heart, the (rattle) of her lungs as she (gasped) for breath, and the (thud) of his boots, echoing through the tunnel behind her.

He knew where she was.

He was coming for her.

The muscles in her legs were screaming in agony but she had no choice. She must run.

⬇ Which column in the table below do you think best describes the writing you crafted in this assessment?

I planned and wrote my story thinking about the effect it would have on the reader.	I planned and wrote my story thinking about how it would grab and hold the reader's interest.	I planned and wrote my story thinking carefully about the effect that the characters, action, language and structure would have on the reader.
I chose some of the language in my story for its effect.	I used quite a wide vocabulary which I chose for effect.	I used a varied range of vocabulary which I chose for effect.
I tried to vary the length and structure of my sentences.	I used a range of sentence structures and lengths and used some of them to achieve specific effects.	I used a varied range of sentence lengths and structures to achieve specific effects.
My speech punctuation is generally accurate and I have tried to use dashes and ellipses for effect.	My speech punctuation is accurate. I have used dashes and ellipses for effect.	My speech punctuation is accurate. I have carefully positioned dashes, ellipses and identifiers to achieve specific effects.

Unit 4
Explain

Have you ever chased cheese down a hill? Charmed worms from the ground? Pulled your strangest face in a gurning competition? Hurled a Wellington boot through the air or pretended to be a warrior in a fantasy battle scene? In this unit you will learn how to write to inform and explain for different audiences by exploring some of the unusual activities some people carry out in their spare time. The texts and activities will help you to make language choices about how to convey and structure information and alter the tone you use in order to explain, inform and entertain in your own writing.

Learning objective

- Understand what is meant by an information text and an explanation text

Information texts give the reader facts, not opinions. For example, the text below gives the reader some facts about balls.

Like information texts, explanation texts also provide the reader with factual information, but in addition to facts they give the reader reasons **how** and **why** actions, events or situations have occurred. For example, the text opposite gives some information about unusual sports and pastimes and explains **how** they are played.

Home | World | UK | England | N Ireland | Scotland | Wales

Video | Current affairs | Blogs | Images | Your feedback

Facts about balls!

1. A table tennis ball, when dropped from 30 cm, should, by international rules, bounce 23 cm high.
2. The world record for the number of tennis balls held in a dog's mouth is five.
3. Under the official rules of snooker, the referee shall, if a player is colour blind, tell him the colour of a ball if requested.
4. In the early 14th century, King Edward II banned football in London because of the great noise caused by 'hustling over large balls, from which many evils may arise'.
5. The world's largest ball of string, in Cawker City, Kansas, measures over 38 ft in circumference.
6. If the Sun were the size of a beach ball, Jupiter would be a golf ball and the Earth would be a pea.
7. Volleyball was invented in 1895 by William G Morgan, who called it Mintonette.
8. There are two golf balls on the Moon, both hit by Alan Shepard on 6 February 1971.

Out of the box, into the wild
Unusual sports that are gaining popularity

Fans of Harry Potter have adopted the fictional sport of Quidditch as 'Muggle Quidditch' and play it in nearly 200 American universities. But stacked up against some of the other unusual sports that are gaining popularity all over the world, playing catch with a broomstick is rather tame. Here are five innovative games that take 'sports' to a new level.

Sheep counting

Approximately 400 sheep dash past ten competitors who try and count them as accurately as possible. The first National Sheep Counting Championships were held in New South Wales, Australia in 2002. Peter Desailly of Australia beat 100 other entrants by correctly counting 277 sheep.

Worm charming

Contestants are required to attract as many worms as possible from the patch of ground assigned to them. Any method can be used, barring the use of dishwashing detergent. The World Worm Charming Championship is now an annual affair in England. A 10-year-old girl set the world record in 2009 when she managed to 'charm' 567 worms from the soil.

Cheese rolling

The Cooper's Hill Cheese-Rolling and Wake is an annual event held near Gloucester in England. Competitors chase a round of Double Gloucester cheese downhill. The first person to cross the finish line at the bottom of the hill is declared the champion and wins the cheese. It can be a dangerous sport for the competitors as well as the audience: those chasing usually sprain their ankles running downhill, but the round of cheese can reach up to 112 km/hr and injure spectators.

Extreme ironing

Advertised as 'the latest danger sport that combines the thrills of an extreme outdoor activity with the satisfaction of a well-pressed shirt', extreme ironing was invented in England in 1997 when Leicester resident Phil Shaw decided to merge his love for adventure sports and his need to sort out laundry. Participants take their ironing boards, clothing and irons anywhere: under a frozen lake or in the middle of the street and even iron while water skiing or snowboarding.

Bed racing

The annual Knaresborough Bed Race began in 1965. Each year the competitors race in teams of six, plus one on the bed. Competitors run along with the bed for 3 km, climb up a hill and then must run down towards the Nidd river and cross it. The team provides their own bed, decorated in the theme for the year.

Activity 1

1   What do the information and explanation texts on pages 48 and 49 have in common? How are they different? Think about:

- their structure – how is each text organised?
- the kinds of information each gives the reader – look in particular at each text's use of **proper nouns** and numbers
- the purpose of each text – how would you expect the reader to react to each of them?

2   Look at the list of texts below.

a   Online encyclopaedia
b   School textbook
c   Dictionary
d   Menu

e   Recipe book
f   Weather forecast
g   Facebook profile
h   Magazine advertisement

Which are:

- information texts
- explanation texts

- both
- neither?

> A **proper noun** is the name of a particular person, place or title, always beginning with a capital letter

Introduction

This section aims to encourage you to develop your reading skills in response to a range of texts. The teaching, texts, activities and tips are all focused on helping you improve your reading skills.

This part of your course encourages you to look at the range and use of media and non-fiction texts. These texts appear everywhere in daily life and the selection in this book should help you to see and appreciate how the English language is presented and used. The texts chosen in this book also aim to improve your reading skills.

Reading media and non-fiction texts is something you do every day without necessarily realising it. This book will help contribute to your understanding, enjoyment and analyses of texts.

The skills that you will work on in this book can be applied to any texts that you read, whether these are in print form or onscreen. You don't just have to rely on English lessons to practise these skills.

This book focuses on the skills that you need to be successful in the exam. You will find a wide range of different kinds of texts and activities based around the sorts of questions that you might get in the exam.

Assessment Objectives

The Assessment Objectives underpin everything you will learn about and be tested upon. It is vital that you understand what these are asking of you. So, here are the Assessment Objectives that relate to your Reading exam together with comments to help you understand what they are.

This Assessment Objective is asking you to show that you:
- understand what you read
- answer the question by selecting appropriate material from the text to support the points that you make
- select texts when asked, from which

Ham, Turkey, Lettuce & Relish   2·40   2·65   2·80
Turkey   1·95   2·15   2·30
Turkey, Stuffing & Cranberry   2·35   2·60   2·75
Bacon   2·25   2·45   2·60
Bacon Lettuce & Tomato   2·35   2·55   2·70
Chicken Mayo & Lettuce   2·00   2·20   2·35
Chicken Tikka & Lettuce   2·05   2·25   2·40
Mexican Chicken   2·05   2·25   2·40

DERIVATIVES **philosophic** adj. **philos**
philosophize (also **-ise**) ● v. theoriz
tal or serious issues, especially ted
argue in terms of one's philosophica
– DERIVATIVES **philosophizer** n.
philosophy ● n. (pl. **-ies**) **1** the stud
nature of knowledge, reality, and ex
ories of a particular philosopher. **2**
etical basis of a branch of knowle
theory or attitude that guides one'
– ORIGIN ME: from OFr. philosop
philosophia 'love of wisdom'.

Quick chickpea pasta

Wholesome, hearty and quick, this is a lovely store-cupboard supper just as it is. Or you could jazz it up a little if you like, perhaps adding some frozen petits pois along with the chickpeas, or some chopped fresh herbs at the end.

SERVES 2
350g small pasta shapes, such as orecchiette or conchigliette
400g tin chickpeas, drained and rinsed
3 tablespoons olive oil
1 garlic clove, sliced
1 red chilli, deseeded and finely chopped
A good squeeze of lemon juice
Sea salt and freshly ground black pepper
Parmesan, hard goat's cheese or other well-flavoured hard cheese, grated, to serve

Bring a pan of water to the boil, salt it well, then add the pasta and cook according to the packet instructions. About 2 minutes before the end, add the chickpeas to the pan, to heat through with the pasta.

Meanwhile, heat the olive oil in a small pan over a very gentle heat. Add the garlic and chilli and cook very gently for 2–3 minutes, without letting the garlic colour. Remove from the heat.

Drain the pasta and chickpeas well. Stir in the garlic, chilli and oil. Add salt and pepper and a good squeeze of lemon juice, to taste. Serve topped with plenty of grated cheese.

Chickpeas with cumin and spinach

This delicately spiced quickie is very good with some warm pitta or flatbreads.

SERVES 2
2 teaspoons sunflower or rapeseed oil

Heat the oil in a saucepan over a medium-low heat. Add the onion and sweat gently for about 8 minutes, stirring occasionally, till tender and golden. Add the garlic, chilli, cumin and lemon zest and cook for another 1–2 minutes.

Activity 2

1 Look again at this extract from the article on page 49 (right).

Choose another extract from the article about a different sport. Annotate the heading and the sentences in your chosen extract like the annotated extract on the right, noting the function of each part of the extract.

2 Choose an unusual sport or hobby that you know about, or make one up. Produce a piece of writing for a news website about your chosen sport, entitled *Top Five Facts About _____*. Look carefully at the article *Facts about balls!* on page 48 to help you.

3 a Look again at the extract on cheese rolling on the right. Now write a similar text about the unusual sport you wrote about in question 2. Write three or four sentences, giving the reader relevant information and explanations of how the sport is played. Make sure that:

- your informative sentences tell the reader **what** your chosen sport is called, and **when** and **where** it takes place, as well as any other relevant or interesting information
- you explain **how** and/or **why** your chosen sport is played and won.

b Annotate your writing with notes like the ones you made in question 1 above, showing the function of each part of your writing.

Cheese rolling

The Cooper's Hill Cheese-Rolling and Wake is an annual event held near Gloucester in England. Competitors chase a round of Double Gloucester cheese downhill. The first person to cross the finish line at the bottom of the hill is declared the champion and wins the cheese. It can be a dangerous sport for the competitors as well as the audience: those chasing usually sprain their ankles running downhill, but the round of cheese can reach up to 112 km/hr and injure spectators.

Information to guide the reader: what this section of the text is about

Topic sentence gives key information about when and where the event takes place

Explanation of how this sport is played and won

Further information about the dangers of this sport

2 Instruct

Learning objective

- Understand how to use imperatives, adverbial phrases and ellipsis to write clear, concise instructions

One of the simplest forms of explanation text is a set of instructions – they explain **how to do something**. Written instructions are not always necessary, however, when pictures can do all the explaining.

How to tie a tie

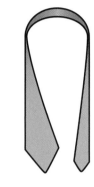

Activity 1

Look at the instruction text below.

STEP 1: The 6 Stack
UP STACKING

The fastest way to build a 6 stack is called the 3-2-1 method. Learn this method and practise it over and over.

Start with 6 cups.

Pick up 3 cups in right hand first and then 2 in left leaving 1.

TIP: When picking up more than one cup, hold cups loose with pinky under bottom cup. Spread cups apart with fingers.

Release bottom cup in right hand to right of centre cup. Release bottom cup from left hand to left of centre cup. Three cups now form the base of your pyramid.

TIP: Alternate your hands "Right, left, right, left, right."

Release next cup in right hand on top of centre and right cups that form base. Set cup in left hand next to it. Set last cup (in right hand) on top.

Place hands around sides of cups as shown.

TIP: Dow
Move 1: S
Move 2: P

Sport stacking is a competitive sport for players of all ages; competitions are held all around the world and hosted by the World Sport Stacking Association in Denver, Colorado.

DOWN STACKING

...e time, slide down ...th right hand, and ...with left hand.

Pick up 3 cups in right hand and 2 cups in left and put them back in one stack of 6.

There you have it. Now ...

PRACTISE! PRACTISE! PRACTISE!

...e 6 in just two moves. ...ands down and out at same time. ...s and place on centre at same time.

1 How have the writer and designer of this text tried to make it easier and clearer for the reader to understand how to do the six stack? Think about:

- the words
- the images
- the presentation and layout.

WRITER'S WORKSHOP: Making your instructions clear

How can I write clear instructions?

1 Sentence functions

Sentences have four basic functions. Each function can be useful when writing instructions.

a A statement: a declaration of fact or opinion. You can use statements to give the reader information:

> The fastest way to build a 6-stack is called the 3-2-1 method.

b A question: a request for information or action, usually requiring a response. You can use questions as subheadings to organise instructions:

> What is the 3-2-1 method?

c An exclamation: an expression of delight or anger or other strong emotion. You can use exclamations to create a sense of enthusiasm in your instructions:

> Kids love sport stacking!

d An **imperative**: an order or command. You will use a lot of these in order to give the reader direct instructions:

> Pick up three cups in right hand.

2 Imperatives

Imperative sentences are a key feature of instructions. Imperative sentences always contain an **imperative verb** giving an order:

> Eat!   ▇ imperative verb

An imperative sentence can also feature a **noun phrase** as the **object** of the verb:

> Eat your dinner!
> ▇ imperative verb
> ▇ this noun phrase is the object of the verb – the verb is commanding you to eat it

The imperative verb can be modified with **adverbs** or **adverbials**:

> Eat your dinner quietly!   ▇ imperative verb   ▇ object   ▇ adverb of manner

Imperatives can sound aggressive.

> Be quiet!   Sit on the chair!

But when you are writing instructions, you can use them to explain to the reader how to do something:

> Start with 6 cups.

> Pick up 3 cups in right hand first and then 2 in left leaving 1.

▇ imperative verbs

3 Clarifying with adverbs and adverbial phrases

You can add further information to your instructions with adverbs and adverbials.

> Pick up 3 cups in right hand first and then 2 in left leaving 1.

These **adverbial phrases** of manner tell you **how** you should do what the imperative is telling you to do.

These adverbs of time tell you **the order** in which you should do what the imperative verb is telling you to do.

4 Keeping it short with ellipsis

Instructions often use ellipsis; the writer misses out the less important words.

> Pick up 3 cups in right hand first and then 2 in left leaving 1.

Why do you think the writer decided to leave these words out?

The instruction, left, could have been written like this:

> Pick up 3 cups in *your* right hand first and then *pick up 2 cups* in *your* left *hand* leaving 1 *on the table*.

Activity 2

1 Write a set of instructions, explaining to the reader how to do something. It could be:

- how to do a particular move in a sport that you play
- how to cook something simple like a piece of toast or a boiled egg
- something else where you have to follow a series of steps in a particular order.

Aim to:

- use imperative sentences to give direct instructions
- modify your choice of imperative verbs with adverbs and adverbial phrases of time, manner or place to clarify the instructions
- use ellipsis to squeeze as much information into your instructions as possible.

CHECK YOUR WRITING

Look back at your writing from Activity 2. Annotate your instructions to show some of the decisions you have made. It might look something like this:

> Take two slices of bread out of bread packet.
>
> Place them in toaster.
>
> Carefully press lever to lower bread into toaster.

Imperative verbs give instructions

Adverbial phrases add important information

Adverb of manner modifies imperative verb

Ellipsis used here – 'the' has been omitted

What do better writers do?

Better writers:

- aim to make their instructions as clear and concise as possible. They do this by using imperative sentences, including adverbs and adverbial phrases of time, manner and place to explain in what order and how each instruction should be followed
- can also use ellipsis to keep their instructions concise. However, they are very careful to keep their meaning as clear as possible, even when they miss out some less important words.

3 Inside information

Learning objective

- Understand how writers use the key features of information texts to create an appropriate tone

Information texts have one key purpose: to pass information on to the reader. They aim to do this as clearly, concisely and engagingly as possible.

Activity 1

Look at the text below. It has been adapted from a website which aims to give its readers information.

How did sport stacking begin?

Sport stacking (also known as cup stacking and speed stacking) was invented at a youth recreation centre in the early 1980s in southern California and received national attention in 1990 on the *Tonight Show*. That was where it first captured the imagination of Bob Fox, who was then a primary school teacher in Colorado.

How did sport stacking become so popular?

Speed Stacks® founder Bob Fox says, "When I first became passionate about sport stacking, a lot of people would hear about it and scratch their heads. Stacking a sport? The only way to explain it was to show them first-hand."

In 1998, Speed Stacks, Inc. was born as a small home business designed to promote sport stacking. It was then that sport stacking spread nationally. Bob started travelling across the country to present stacking to fellow PE teachers and in 2000, after 17 years of teaching, he decided to leave his school to devote himself full-time to sport stacking with Speed Stacks®. The sport's popularity continues to grow. More than 38,718 schools worldwide have a Speed Stacks® sport stacking programme as part of their PE curriculum.

What are the benefits of sport stacking?

A university study by Dr Brian Udermann, currently at the University of Wisconsin-Lacrosse, confirms that sport stacking improves hand-eye coordination and reaction time by up to 30 percent.

Stacking helps train the brain for other sports and activities where the use of both hands is important, such as playing a musical instrument or using a computer. Sequencing and patterning are also elements of sport stacking, which can help with reading and maths skills.

A world record!

In 2013, a Guinness World Record was set for the number of people sport stacking at different locations in one day. 555,932 stackers from 29 countries stacked cups for at least 30 minutes and raised a lot of money for good causes at the same time!

1 Check how much information you have picked up from the text by answering these questions.

   a Where was sport stacking invented?
   b What are two of the benefits of sport stacking?
   c What is the world record for the number of people stacking at different locations in one day?

2 How has the writer tried to make it easier and clearer for the reader to gather information from this text?

WRITER'S WORKSHOP: Setting the tone

An information text should be clear, concise, reliable and accurate. To make the reader feel that your information text is reliable, you should aim to give your writing an authoritative, formal tone.

Which tense should I write in?

When writing information about events that have happened in the past, you should use the **past tense**:

Sport stacking (also known as cup stacking and speed stacking) was invented at a youth recreation centre in the early 1980s.

verb in past tense

When writing information about the current situation, you should write in the **present tense**:

sport stacking improves hand-eye coordination and reaction time by up to 30 percent.

verb in present tense

Try rewriting the sentence above in the past tense. What effect does it have?

Should I write in the first person or the third person?

Writing in the **first person** (I, me, we, our) suggests that the writer is writing about a personal experience and giving a personal opinion.

Information texts are usually written in the **third person**. It suggests that the information given in the text is factual, impartial and reliable. Compare these two versions of a sentence taken from the web article on the opposite page:

> Stacking helps train the brain for other sports and activities where the use of both hands is important.

> I think that stacking helps train the brain for other sports and activities where the use of both hands is important.
>
> written in the first person

Which sounds more formal and authoritative? How might the reader respond differently to the sentence written in the first person?

How can I choose language that makes my information writing sound more reliable and authoritative?

Information writing focuses on factual detail and often uses more **formal language** choices to express it. This adds to the overall impression that the text is a reliable and trustworthy source of information.

For example, which of the two pieces of information below do you think a reader would feel was more reliable?

> Sport stacking... received national attention in 1990 on the *Tonight Show*.

> Back in the day, sport stacking got really well known all over the place when it was on the telly.

History of football:
* Ball games played by Ancient Greeks and Romans
* Cuju or Tsu' Chu (means kick ball) played in Ancient China with leather ball stuffed with hair and feathers
* Loads of different versions of football played around UK since 8th century
* Rulebook found for ancient version: any number of players had to boot ball over fields/hedges/fences/stream/woodland to get to other side's village. Teams could do anything to stop other side – except murder
* Modern football started 1863 – 11 football clubs got together and formed Football Association.
* First FA Cup in 1872. Just 15 clubs entered
* First women's football match played 1895 – now the most popular female team sport in UK

Activity 2

1 Write the first two or three paragraphs of a web article giving information on the history of football. You can use some or all of the facts from the notes on the left and you could add some facts you already know. Make sure that the tone of your writing is formal and authoritative.

What do better writers do?

Better writers:

* use tense consistently. They write consistently in the present tense when writing about current information. They write consistently in the past tense when writing about events which have already happened
* use the third person and make more formal language choices when they want their writing to have an impartial and authoritative tone.

- Understand what is meant by the active and passive voices
- Understand how to use the passive voice to focus the reader on key information

The writer of an information text needs to provide reliable, trustworthy information, and can make choices which help it sound more reliable **and** focus the reader on the key facts.

Things you never knew about Worm Charming!

The Worm Charming event was first devised by Mr John Bailey, who was the deputy headmaster of Willaston County Primary School, Nantwich, Cheshire from 1961 to 1983.

It was designed as a fund-raising event incorporated into our School Fete in 1980.

The rules were compiled by John Bailey in 1980 but over the years the size of plots has been increased from three yards square to three metres square to bring us in line with EEC requirements.

We have also increased the number of squares from 100 to 144 to accommodate additional competitors who compete on behalf of various charities.

The first Worm Charming World Record was set in 1980 by Mr Tom Shufflebotham who raised 511 worms from a three-yards-square plot. This remained unbroken until 2009, when Miss S and Mr M Smith charmed an incredible 567 worms from their plot!

Because of fierce local competition and all year round training by worm-charming fanatics, the trophy had never left the village of Willaston until, in 1996, father and son team Phil and David Williams from Wiltshire won the competition with a total of 157 worms.

The most successful method used so far is that of hand vibrating a four tine garden fork inserted approximately 15 cms into the turf, now known locally in South Cheshire as 'twanging'.

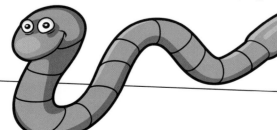

Activity 1

The World Worm Charming Championships take place every year in the village of Willaston in Cheshire. Read the text opposite, taken from the World Worm Charming Championships website.

1   a   How would you describe the main purpose of this text? Choose one purpose from the suggestions below.

inform	entertain	explain	describe	persuade

argue	advise	analyse	review

   b   Does the text have any secondary purposes? Choose at least one from the suggestions above.

2   a   How would you describe the **tone** of this text? Choose two or three words from the suggestions below or add your own.

humorous	serious	formal	aggressive	neutral

melancholy	mocking	**sinister**	informal	dramatic

   b   How has the writer of this text achieved this tone? Explain your ideas, using a quotation from the text to support each one.

> **Glossary**
>
> **melancholy:** sad, depressing
>
> **sinister:** implying that something bad is going to happen

WRITER'S WORKSHOP: The active and passive voices

How can I use the passive voice to focus my reader on key information?

There are two voices in English: the active and the passive.

The active voice uses a sentence structure in which the subject of the sentence either:

- does something or
- does something to the object of the sentence.

For example:

In the passive voice the object of the active verb becomes the subject of the passive verb:

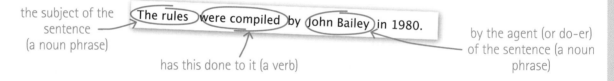

Using the passive voice means that the writer does not have to reveal the agent of the sentence. The agent can be omitted. For example:

Using the passive voice can:

- focus the reader's attention on key information by making it the subject of the sentence
- avoid naming the agent if the writer feels that the reader does not need to know that information
- weaken your writing by allowing you to omit essential or interesting information – so beware of using the passive voice!

How can I alter the emphasis of my writing?

Look at these examples of the passive voice from the worm-charming web page:

> The Worm Charming event was first devised by Mr John Bailey, who was the deputy headmaster of Willaston County Primary School, Nantwich, Cheshire from 1961 to 1983.

> It was designed as a fund-raising event incorporated into our School Fete in 1980.

> the size of plots has been increased from three yards square to three metres square

Try rewriting each sentence in the active voice and comparing the two versions. What different effects does each version of each sentence have?

Activity 2

1 Look at the instruction text you wrote in Activity 2 on page 55. Have you used the passive voice in any of your sentences? If so, what effect does it have?

2 Choose two sentences from your text that you have written in the active voice.

  a Experiment with rewriting both of them in the passive voice. Try omitting the agent.

  b What effect does it have, with and without the agent? Write a sentence or two explaining your ideas.

What do better writers do?

Better writers use both the active and passive voices. They use the active voice much more frequently, but choose to use the passive voice occasionally to alter the emphasis or focus of their writing. They are especially careful not to omit important or interesting information when using the passive voice.

5 Building up your sentences 1

Learning objectives

- Understand how simple sentences can be developed to give the reader detailed information
- Understand how coordinate clauses and coordinating conjunctions can link ideas to make information and explanation as clear as possible

1 In how many different sentence structures can you convey all this information to a reader? For example, can you write it in:

- four sentences
- two sentences
- three sentences
- one sentence?

Experiment to try creating as many different sentence structures as you can. You could try replacing some of the **nouns** with **pronouns** and adding adverbs such as 'first', 'next' and 'finally', to help make the information as clear as possible.

2 Look at all the different ways in which you have written the above information.

a Which version sounds best?

b Which version do you prefer? Write a sentence or two explaining your choice.

When you are informing or explaining to your reader, you have to think about the best way to structure your sentences to convey information as clearly as possible.

Activity 1

Look at the information about the Knaresborough Bed Race below.

Competitors:
- run along with the bed for 3 km
- push the bed up a hill
- push the bed down the hill
- get the bed across the River Nidd.

WRITER'S WORKSHOP: Structuring sentences to make information text as clear as possible

How should I use simple sentences to convey information clearly?

A **simple sentence** consists of one **main clause** which contains one **main verb**. It describes just one event or action. However, there are lots of ways in which further information can be added.

Look at the sentence below. It is from the web article *Out of the box, into the wild* on page 49. It is a simple sentence – it contains just one verb – but lots of information has been added using adjectives and adverbial phrases:

> The first National Sheep Counting Championships were held in New South Wales, Australia in 2002.

	adjectives		noun		main verb

	adverbial phrase of place – tells you where it took place

	adverbial phrase of time – tells you when it took place

- How much information can you remove from the simple sentence above before it stops being a sentence?
- How much detailed information can you add to the simple sentence above without adding another verb? You will need to make the information up!

How should I use coordinate clauses to link information?

Coordinating conjunctions include:
- and
- but
- or
- so

You can link the information in simple sentences by joining them together with a **conjunction**.

For example, you can use **coordinating conjunctions** such as 'and' or 'but'. Clauses joined with a coordinating conjunction are known as **coordinate clauses**.

Look at another sentence from the *Out of the box, into the wild* text on page 49. Two clauses have been joined together with the coordinating conjunction 'and':

> The first person to cross the finish line at the bottom of the hill is declared the champion and wins the cheese.

	coordinate clause 1
	coordinating conjunction
	coordinate clause 2

The writer could have written it as two simple sentences:

> The first person to cross the finish line at the bottom of the hill is declared the champion. They win the cheese.

Read both versions aloud: the original version which uses a coordinating conjunction and the rewritten version consisting of two simple sentences.

- Which one sounds better?
- Which version do you prefer – the original version or the rewritten version? Write a sentence or two explaining your choice.

How else can I use coordinate clauses?

You can join more than one coordinate clause with commas and coordinating conjunctions. Look at another sentence from *Out of the box, into the wild*:

> Competitors run along with the bed for 3 km, climb up a hill and then must run down towards the Nidd river and cross it.

The writer could have chosen to write this sentence as four simple sentences. For example:

> Competitors run along with the bed for 3 km. They climb up a hill.
> They then must run down towards the Nidd river. They cross it.

Read both versions aloud: the original version which uses a coordinating conjunction and the rewritten version made up of two simple sentences.

- Which one sounds better?
- Which version do you prefer – the original version or the rewritten version? Write a sentence or two explaining your choice.

	coordinate clause 1
	coordinate clause 2
	coordinating conjunction
	coordinate clause 3
	coordinate clause 4
	comma used to separate two coordinate clauses in a list

What do better writers do?

Better writers choose from a variety of sentence structures to convey information as clearly as possible. These include:

- simple sentences, featuring adjectives and adverbial phrases to add detailed information
- coordinate clauses and coordinating conjunctions to express the relationship between two pieces of information.

Activity 2

1 Look at the notes below. They are all facts about the unusual sport of welly wanging.

- The object of the sport of welly wanging is to throw a wellington boot as far as possible.
- 'Wanging' is a Yorkshire word for 'throwing'.
- The Official World Welly Wanging Championships are held in the village of Upperthong in Yorkshire.
- All contestants have to throw a Dunlop size 9 green non-steel-toecap wellington boot.
- The contestant can choose whether it's a right or left boot.
- Winners of the adults' championship receive a trophy.
- Winners of the children's championship receive a five-pound note.

a To get ready to write about welly wanging, decide on the best order in which to use these facts.

b Write a short informative text about welly wanging using only simple sentences. Remember: simple sentences contain only one clause and one verb. They describe just one event or action.

c Rewrite your text about welly wanging using a variety of simple sentences and coordinate clauses joined with coordinating conjunctions. Aim to:

- experiment with where and how you join your simple sentences
- make your writing as clear and informative as possible.

6 Building up your sentences 2

Learning objective

- Understand how to form subordinate and relative clauses and use them to add clear, detailed information to your writing

You can add more variety to your sentence structures with **subordinate clauses** and **relative clauses**.

Activity 1

Look at the information about Worm Charming below.

- John Bailey first devised the Worm Charming event.
- Worm Charming was devised as a fund-raising event.
- John Bailey was the deputy headmaster of the local primary school.
- John Bailey compiled the rules of the Worm Charming event.
- It was won by local people from 1980 to 1995.
- In 1996 it was won by a team from Wiltshire.

1 In how many different sentence structures can you convey this information to a reader? For example, can you write it in:

- four sentences
- three sentences
- two sentences
- one sentence?

Experiment to try creating as many different sentence structures as you can.

2 Look at all the different ways in which you have written the above information.

a Which version sounds best?

b Which version do you prefer? Write a sentence or two explaining your choice.

WRITER'S WORKSHOP: Linking information with subordinate and relative clauses

How do I use subordinate clauses and subordinating conjunctions?

Subordinating conjunctions include:

• although • as • when • whenever • if • because • unless • while • until • whereas

One way to link two pieces of related information is with a **subordinating conjunction**. For example, look at these two simple sentences:

> *A 10-year-old girl set the world record in 2009. She managed to 'charm' 567 worms from the soil.*

The writer of the article on page 49 decided to link them with a subordinating conjunction:

A 10-year-old girl set the world record in 2009 **when** she managed to 'charm' 567 worms from the soil.

main clause — subordinating conjunction and part of subordinate clause — subordinate clause

Read both versions aloud: the original version which uses a subordinating conjunction and the version made up of two simple sentences.

- Which one sounds better?
- Which version do you prefer? Write a sentence or two explaining your choice.

Subordinating conjunctions like 'when' and 'until' add information about time to main clauses: when, and for how long, something happened.

How can subordinating conjunctions help convey information clearly?

Other subordinating conjunctions can express a range of relationships between main and subordinate clauses. For example, in the sentence below, the subordinating conjunction 'because' indicates a cause – the reason why the trophy had never left the village of Willlaston.

Because of fierce local competition and all year round training by worm-charming fanatics, the trophy had never left the village of Willaston until, in 1996, father and son team Phil and David Williams from Wiltshire won the competition with a total of 157 worms.

Subordinate clauses and main clauses can often be swapped around without altering the sense of a sentence. The three clauses in the sentence above are shown below:

Because of fierce local competition and all year round training by worm-charming fanatics,	the trophy had never left the village of Willaston	until, in 1996, father and son team Phil and David Williams from Wiltshire won the competition with a total of 157 worms.

- In how many different ways can you organise the three clauses in this sentence?
- Which version sounds better?
- Which version is clearer?
- Why do you think the writer chose to structure this sentence in this way?

How do I use relative pronouns and relative clauses to expand noun phrases, adding more detail?

You can add further information to your sentence by using a relative clause to modify a noun phrase:

the noun phrase 'ten competitors' can be expanded by adding this relative clause, which then becomes part of the noun phrase

> Approximately 400 sheep dash past ten competitors who try and count them as accurately as possible.

	main clause
	relative pronoun
	relative clause

the noun 'William G Morgan' is modified by adding this relative clause to create a noun phrase

> Volleyball was invented in 1895 by William G Morgan, who called it Mintonette.

	main clause
	relative pronoun
	relative clause

Relative clauses are linked to main clauses with **relative pronouns** such as:

> **that**   **which**   **who**   **whose**

- How could you restructure the sentences above using simple sentences?
- Why do you think the writers chose to structure these sentences using a main clause and a relative clause instead of writing them as two simple sentences?

What do better writers do?

Better writers:

- choose from a variety of sentence structures to convey information as clearly as possible

- use subordinate clauses linked with subordinating conjunctions to express the relationship between two pieces of information as clearly as possible

- use relative clauses to expand noun phrases, adding essential or engaging information.

Activity 2

Look again at the writing you completed in Activity 2 on page 65. Now look at some more facts about the sport of welly wanging:

> There are lots of different techniques for welly wanging including one-handed, two-handed or backwards throws.
>
> The people of Upperthong believe the sport was invented in their village.
>
> Welly-wanging events now take place all over the UK.
>
> Boot-throwing events also take place in Germany, Finland, Poland and New Zealand.

1 Referring back to the facts on page 65, rewrite your text about welly wanging using a variety of sentence structures, including:

- simple sentences
- subordinate clauses
- coordinate clauses
- relative clauses.

Aim to:

- experiment with where and how you join your simple sentences
- make your writing as clear and informative as possible.

CHECK YOUR WRITING

Look back at your writing in Activity 2.

➡ Annotate your writing, identifying all the different sentence structures you have used and the reasons you chose them.

⬇ Look at the table below and your writing from Activity 2. Tick the column you think describes your writing.

I used some developed simple sentences to give the reader information, and I linked some information using coordinate and subordinate clauses and conjunctions.	I used a variety of developed simple sentences, relative clauses, coordinate and subordinate clauses and conjunctions. I chose some sentence structures intentionally to convey information clearly to the reader.	I used a variety of developed simple sentences, relative clauses, coordinate and subordinate clauses and conjunctions. I carefully chose each sentence's structure to convey information clearly to the reader.

7 Language choices

Learning objective

- Understand how to choose vocabulary which is appropriate to your topic and your audience

Glossary

BTEC: stands for Business and Technology Education Council – a vocational qualification

Communicating clearly with your reader is an essential part of writing information and explanation texts. Choosing the right language for your audience is one of the most important decisions a writer has to make.

Activity 1

Read the text below. It is taken from a sports science textbook for **BTEC** students. It explains some of the injuries that can occur when playing sport.

BTEC Sports Science

Sprains and strains

Many people find it difficult to differentiate between a sprain and a strain. An understanding of basic anatomy makes it easy to tell the difference:

- a **sprain** is damage to ligaments (stretch or tear)
- a **strain** is damage to muscle or tendon.

Sprain

The causes of a sprain are generally a sudden twist, impact or fall that makes the joint move outside its normal range of movement. Sprains commonly occur to the ankle, wrist, thumb or knee.

Strain

A strain is damage to a muscle or tendon caused by overstretching that particular area. Similar to a sprain, a strain can result in a simple overstretching of the muscle or, in more serious examples, partial or even complete rupture.

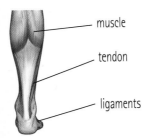

muscle

tendon

ligaments

Concussion

Concussion is caused by the brain shaking inside the skull. This causes a temporary loss of consciousness or functioning. Other signs and symptoms include:

- partial or complete loss of consciousness, usually of short duration
- shallow breathing
- nausea and vomiting can occur when the person starts to regain consciousness
- headache may occur.

Tendonitis

The repetitive and high-impact nature of sporting activity involves continued muscle actions, pulling on tendons, resulting in movement of the skeleton. The varied and dynamic movements involved in sports can, from time to time, place friction on the tendons causing irritation and inflammation.

This inflammation is called tendonitis, and is generally caused by overuse, particularly with increased or different training demands. The symptoms normally subside within a few days, but without care the problem can last weeks or even months. Typical locations of tendonitis could be the Achilles tendon and within the complex structures of the shoulder joint.

Cramp

Cramp is an involuntary contraction of muscles. Muscles that are particularly susceptible are the gastrocnemius (calf), the quadriceps (thigh), the hamstrings, the abdomen and the feet and hands, depending on the type of activity. Cramp is caused by a lack of oxygen to the muscles, or a lack of water or salt.

---

1 a Which of the key features of an explanation text does this text have?

   - Written in the present tense
   - Written in the third person
   - Written using formal language

   b Choose a short quotation from the text as evidence of these key features, then annotate your quotation to highlight them.

   c How is this text different from those which you have looked at so far in this unit?

2 Look at the way the writer has structured the text.

   a Why has the writer used headings?

   b Why is some text emboldened?

   c Why has the writer set out some of the information using bullet points?

WRITER'S WORKSHOP: Using the right words

How do I choose the right vocabulary for my audience?

The text on page 70 was written for 17–18-year-olds who are studying to achieve a BTEC qualification in Sports Science.

Look carefully at the writer's choice of vocabulary in this section of the text:

> Cramp is an involuntary contraction of muscles. Muscles that are particularly susceptible are the gastrocnemius (calf), the quadriceps (thigh), the hamstrings, the abdomen and the feet and hands, depending on the type of activity.

The writer creates a tone of authority and informs the reader by choosing to use:

- specialist vocabulary: words which are from the **lexical fields** of anatomy and medicine
- formal vocabulary to explain their meaning.

Glossary

lexical field: a group of words or phrases that are all associated with a particular subject or category

1 a Can you identify two examples of specialist vocabulary which the writer has chosen?

b Can you identify two examples of more formal vocabulary which the writer has chosen?

c Try replacing the four words you have identified with choices which are less formal or specialist. What effect have your changes had on the impact of the text?

2 Why do you think the writer has added some extra information in brackets?

3 Look at some of the synonyms and related words which the writer could have chosen to use in this section of the text (see spider diagrams).

a Why do you think the writer chose to use 'involuntary', 'susceptible' and 'abdomen'?

b How might the writer's language choices differ if they were writing for Year 6 students?

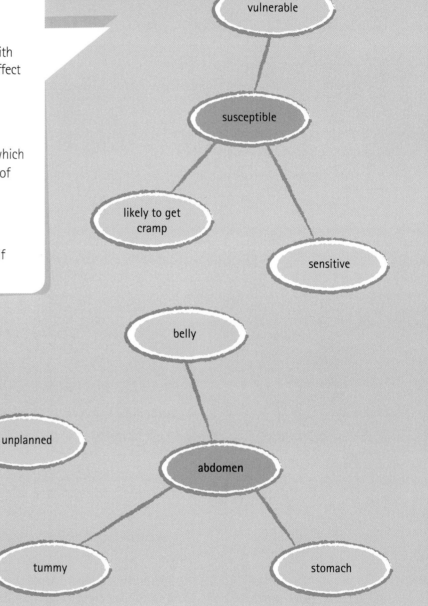

What do better writers do?

Better writers:

- choose vocabulary which is appropriate to their topic and their audience when writing formal information and explanation texts
- select specialist vocabulary to inform the reader and explain their topic
- make formal vocabulary choices which clearly convey information to the intended reader.

Activity 2

1   Look at the information below. It is about bruises.

> Bruise
> - Also called a contusion
> - Blue/purple discoloration of skin as result of trauma caused by impact, surgery, etc.
> - Rupture of small blood vessels (capillaries and venules) beneath skin
> - Blood haemorrhages into soft tissue beneath skin
> - Apply ice for up to 15 minutes to reduce swelling
> - Usually heals within five days

a   Write three or four sentences explaining what a bruise is, when and why it occurs, and how it can be treated. Aim to make your writing appropriate to an audience of 17–18-year-old BTEC students.

b   Rewrite your text on bruises, making it appropriate for an audience of Year 6 students.

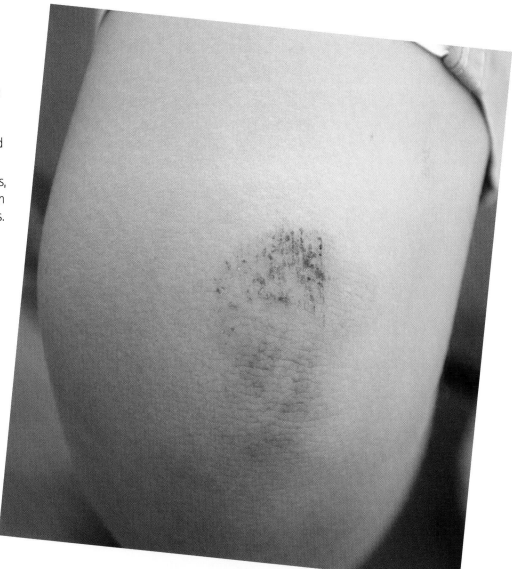

Assessment: Information texts

Learning objective

- Understand how to structure and write a complete information text

So far in this unit, you have explored:

- the key features of information and explanation texts
- the four different functions of a sentence
- using the past and present tense
- writing in the third person and using formal language
- using the active and passive voices

- developing simple sentences to convey detailed information
- linking and developing information using a range of sentence structures including coordinate, subordinate and relative clauses
- choosing vocabulary appropriate to your reader.

In this task, you will need to use all these skills to craft a short information text about a strange or unusual sport or hobby.

PLAN

Follow the steps below to collect your ideas and make important decisions before you start writing.

1 **What will my information text be about?**

Imagine your school or local area holds a strange sporting event each year. It could be a real event or you could make one up. You could reuse the sport you wrote about in Activity 2 on page 51, or come up with a new idea. It could be something to do with:

local wildlife, like the worm-charming championship in Cheshire

local food, like the cheese-rolling race in Gloucestershire

a race, like the Knaresborough Bed Race

or something else

2 **What information should I include in my text?**

Think of some interesting facts about the strange sporting event you have chosen or imagined. They could be about:

the history of the event   the rules of the event   the winners of the event

records set at the event   some other interesting facts

3 **How will I organise my information text?**

You could:

organise your writing using paragraphs like the worm-charming web page on page 58

organise your writing under subheadings like 'Out of the box, into the wild' on page 49

or in a different, original way

4 **What purpose and tone do I want to achieve?**

Informative and neutral?

Informative, entertaining and humorous?

Or something else?

WRITE

You are now ready to write your information text.

REFLECT

Your task

Write the text for a web page which gives the reader information about an unusual or strange sport. Your readers will be adults and young people aged 12+.

Aim to write between 150 and 200 words.

1 When you have completed your information text, read it through carefully. Are you pleased with it? Which items on the checklist do you feel you have achieved, and which could you improve?

2 a Choose one or two areas in your writing which you feel you could improve.

   b Working on your own, or with a partner, look back at the relevant pages in this unit to remind yourself of the choices you could make to improve your writing in those one or two areas.

   c Write a sentence or two explaining **how** you will improve your writing in those one or two areas.

   d Make the improvements you want to make to your writing.

☐ I think I have structured my information text effectively.

☐ I think I have used the appropriate tense consistently and accurately.

☐ I think I have achieved my intended purpose and tone.

☐ I have achieved that tone by selecting either the first or third person, formal or informal language choices, and the active or passive voice.

☐ I have used a range of sentence structures to convey information as clearly as possible.

CHECK YOUR WRITING

⬇ Looking at the table below, decide which column you think best describes the writing you crafted in this assessment.

I planned and wrote my information text, structuring it with subheadings.	I planned and wrote my information text, organising key information under subheadings and/or in paragraphs.	I planned, wrote and structured my information text, selecting information and organising it to achieve my intended purpose and tone.
I used the past and present tenses appropriately but not always consistently.	I used the past and present tenses appropriately and consistently.	I used the past and present tenses appropriately and consistently.
I chose some language thinking about the effect I wanted to have on the reader.	I made language choices which were suitable for my reader and helped me achieve my intended tone. I used the active and passive voices.	I carefully crafted my writing, selecting first or third person, language choices and both active and passive voices to achieve my intended purpose and tone. I chose language which was appropriate for my audience.
	I used a variety of developed simple sentences, relative clauses, coordinate and subordinate clauses and conjunctions. I chose some sentence structures intentionally to convey information clearly to the reader.	I used a variety of developed simple sentences, relative clauses, coordinate and subordinate clauses and conjunctions. I carefully chose each sentence's structure to convey information clearly to the reader.

8 Explaining and storytelling

Learning objective

- Understand how information and explanation texts can be structured to engage the reader

Presenting the reader with a series of facts and explanations is not the only way in which a writer can structure an information or explanation text.

Activity 1

Carefully read the article below. It is taken from a news website.

Home	World	UK	England	N Ireland	Scotland	Wales

Video   Current affairs   Blogs   Images   Your feedback

Have you got the bug for bunnies?

I am at a village hall in Langham, East Anglia, where the Colchester and District Rabbit Club is holding a 'show' – a competition to find the most perfect rabbit. One hundred and thirty cages have been set up for the event, and every one of these is now occupied.

The animals gaze out at me, chewing contentedly. 'There are 50 breeds in the world,' says Eddie Hutchings, one of Britain's leading rabbit judges, 'and 40 of them are represented here.' Are they expensive? After all, show-quality dogs can set you back thousands of pounds. 'Some can be,' says Eddie. 'The big 'uns go for up to 10 quid.'

Pat Gaskins, editor of *Fur and Feather* magazine (which, she says, having been founded in 1856, is the longest running animal magazine in the world), has overheard us talking about money. 'No **fancier** is in it for profit,' she says. 'We're in it for the glory, for the honour. For the passion.' Just as well, really. Today's winner will be awarded the princely sum of £1 (plus a rosette).

Rabbits are jumping in popularity. According to Paul Hopkins, the president elect of the British Rabbit Council, membership has increased from 2,500 to 3,000 in the past 18 months. There are now around 1,500 rabbit shows per year in Britain, each attracting an average of 130 contestants, and these figures are growing all the time.

I meet Mr Hopkins at the judging table. He and his fellow judges are working methodically, picking up rabbits, examining them, scoring them out of a hundred, and returning them to their cages. They are judging in four breed-categories, and also looking for 'best in show'.

'Rabbits are now the third most popular pet in the UK,' he says. 'They are definitely coming back into fashion. Children have been going mad for televisions and computers, but now people are realising that it is better for them to have a pet. It gives them a different attitude to life, and helps them to develop a sense of responsibility.'

Glossary

fancier: someone who has great enthusiasm for, or breeds, a particular species of animal

1 a How would you describe the main purpose of this text? Choose one purpose from the suggestions below.

inform	entertain	explain	describe	persuade

argue	advise	analyse	review

   b Choose a short quotation from the article to support each of your answers to question 1a.

2 Look back and remind yourself of what has been covered so far in this unit.

   a Which language choices has the writer of the text about rabbits used?

   b Why do you think the writer made these decisions? Write two or three sentences explaining your ideas.

Activity 2

1 One way in which the writer of the article on page 76 has engaged and entertained the reader is by recounting the story of their day at a rabbit show.

   Write a summary of each paragraph in his story. For example, you could begin like this:

> *The narrator is at a rabbit show. He chats to one of the judges.*

2 In the article, the writer also includes a lot of information and explanation about rabbit shows and rabbit breeders. Note down at least one piece of information or explanation which the writer includes in each paragraph. You could write your answers alongside your answers to question 1 in a table like the one below:

	The story	Information/explanation
1	The narrator is at a rabbit show	Rabbit shows are held to find the most perfect rabbit
2	He talks to one of the judges	There are 50 breeds of rabbit in the world. Show-quality rabbits can cost £10.
3		

Rabbit show jumping
- Rabbits are encouraged to jump over a series of obstacles.
- It's just like show jumping for horses – but adapted for rabbits.
- The winner is the rabbit that completes the course in the shortest time and with the fewest errors.
- It was invented in Sweden in the early 1980s.
- Rabbit show jumping is known as Kaninhoppning in Sweden.
- The record for the highest rabbit jump is 99.5 cm.
- Rabbit Jumping UK is a group of British rabbit-jumping enthusiasts. They were formed in 2009.
- Experts recommend a rabbit with a long back and long legs as most appropriate for show jumping.
- Lop-eared rabbits are not recommended as they can easily trip over and damage their long floppy ears.

Activity 3

1 Look at the information about the unusual sport of rabbit show jumping opposite.

2 Imagine a news website has asked you to write an article about rabbit show jumping. Your article should:

   • inform readers about this unusual sport
   • explain how and why people take part.

You have spent a day at a rabbit show-jumping event to find out all about it.

Now plan your article, thinking about how you will tell the story of your day, and combine it with information and explanations about the unusual sport of rabbit show jumping. You could note down your ideas in a table like the one in Activity 2 question 2.

> You will need to imagine the conversations you have with the experts, judges and participants you meet and interview during your day at the event.

3 Annotate all the different pieces of information/explanation in your plan to show which will inform readers about rabbit show jumping and which will explain how and why people take part in it.

9 Explaining and engaging

Learning objectives

- Understand ways in which writers can create humour to engage the reader
- Understand some of the ways in which you can use a range of sentence structures to convey information clearly and concisely

The two ways in which a writer can engage the reader are through:

- content choices, e.g. the ideas and information included in a text
- writing choices, e.g. the structure, language, sentence types, etc. used to convey that content.

Activity 1

One of the writer's choices in *Have you got the bug for bunnies?* is to use humour to engage and entertain readers. Look again at these three paragraphs from the article:

> The animals gaze out at me, chewing contentedly. 'There are 50 breeds in the world,' says Eddie Hutchings, one of Britain's leading rabbit judges, 'and 40 of them are represented here.' Are they expensive? After all, show-quality dogs can set you back thousands of pounds. 'Some can be,' says Eddie. 'The big 'uns go for up to 10 quid.'
>
> Pat Gaskins, editor of *Fur and Feather* magazine (which, she says, having been founded in 1856, is the longest-running animal magazine in the world), has overheard us talking about money. 'No fancier is in it for profit,' she says. 'We're in it for the glory, for the honour. For the passion.' Just as well, really. Today's winner will be awarded the princely sum of £1 (plus a rosette).
>
> Rabbits are jumping in popularity. According to Paul Hopkins, the president elect of the British Rabbit Council, membership has increased from 2,500 to 3,000 in the past 18 months. There are now around 1,500 rabbit shows per year in Britain, each attracting an average of 130 contestants, and these figures are growing all the time.

1 Look closely at the first paragraph above. Why do you think the writer has pointed out that 'show-quality dogs can set you back thousands of pounds'? How has the writer used this to create humour?

2 a Look closely at the second paragraph above. Why do you think the writer has described the 'sum of £1' as 'princely'?

  b Why do you think the writer has added the fact that the winner will also win a rosette – and placed it in brackets?

3 Look closely at the third paragraph above. Why do you think the writer has chosen the verb 'jumping' to describe the increasing popularity of rabbits as pets?

WRITER'S WORKSHOP: Sentence structure

How can I use a variety of sentence structures to engage my readers?

You can convey or explain the same information in a variety of different sentence structures.

So far in this unit, you have explored some different ways of structuring sentences using:

- main clauses
- coordinate clauses
- subordinate clauses
- relative clauses.

You can also use non-finite clauses to add or develop detailed information.

How do I use non-finite clauses to add detail to my sentences?

Non-finite clauses are clauses which are linked into sentences with a **non-finite verb**. A non-finite verb is either:

- a **present participle**, which ends in '–ing', such as 'chewing' or 'working'
- a **past participle**, which usually ends in '–ed', such as 'jumped' or 'increased'. There are, however, **irregular past participles** such as 'heard' or 'done'.
- an **infinitive**, the basic form of a verb which sometimes begins with 'to', such as 'to be' or 'to find'.

You can use non-finite clauses to add related information to a sentence. For example:

non-finite verb

The animals gaze out at me, chewing contentedly.

non-finite clause

The writer could have chosen to convey this in two simple sentences:

The animals gaze out at me. They are chewing contentedly.

Using a non-finite clause allows the writer to convey the same information, but more concisely.

How do I decide the best way to structure my sentences?

When you craft sentences, you have to decide when, where and how to use the information you want to include. There are lots of ways to do that, and lots of decisions to be taken.

Look at this sentence from the article, *Have you got the bug for bunnies?*.

Pat Gaskins, editor of *Fur and Feather* magazine (which, she says, having been founded in 1856, is the longest-running animal magazine in the world), has overheard us talking about money.

In this sentence, there are four pieces of information.

The sentence tells the reader that:

1 | Pat Gaskins | | has overheard us talking about money. |

This is the main clause in the sentence, with 'talking about money' as a non-finite clause. All the other details in this sentence could be omitted and the sentence would still make sense.

2 | Pat Gaskins | is | the editor of *Fur and Feather* magazine. |

This is conveyed as a **noun phrase in apposition** – which means that the proper noun 'Pat Gaskins' is post-modified by the noun phrase 'the editor of *Fur and Feather* magazine'. News and magazine journalists often use nouns in apposition like this to give details about someone they are quoting.

3 The non-finite clause | having been founded in 1856 | tells the reader when the magazine was first published.

4 | which, she says | | is the longest-running animal magazine in the world |

This, with the relative pronoun 'which', is a relative clause.

The writer could have decided to connect all four pieces of information using more relative clauses. For example:

| Pat Gaskins | | who is the editor of Fur and Feather magazine, | | which was founded in 1856, |

| which she says makes it the longest-running animal magazine in the world, | | overhears us talking about money. |

Why do you think the writer decided not to use lots of relative clauses?

The writer could have used lots of non-finite clauses:

| Pat Gaskins | | being editor of Fur and Feather magazine, | | founded in 1856, |

| making it the longest-running animal magazine in the world, | | overhears us talking about money. |

Why do you think the writer decided not to use lots of non-finite clauses?

The writer could have used some subordinate and coordinate clauses:

| Pat Gaskins is the editor of Fur and Feather magazine, | | and overhears us talking about money. |

| This is the longest-running animal magazine in the world, | | as it was founded in 1856. |

Why do you think the writer decided not to use some subordinate and coordinate clauses?

Activity 2

1 a Experiment with writing two or three different versions of the sentence you explored in the Writer's Workshop opposite. You could use any combination of:

- a relative clause
- a non-finite clause
- a subordinate or coordinate clause
- a noun phrase in apposition.

   b Which of the different versions you have written do you prefer? Why?
      Write a sentence or two explaining your choice.

2 Look again at the original version of the sentence from the article on page 76:

> Pat Gaskins, editor of *Fur and Feather* magazine (which, she says, having been founded in 1856, is the longest-running animal magazine in the world), has overheard us talking about money.

   a Why do you think the writer of the article decided to put the relative clause and non-finite clause inside brackets?

   b Could you improve any of your versions of this sentence by placing one or more of the clauses in brackets?

3 On page 77, you planned a text about rabbit show-jumping. Using your plan, write the opening paragraphs of a short article informing and explaining to your reader all about this unusual sport. Aim to write around 150–200 words and:

- use humour to engage and entertain the reader
- use a variety of clause and sentence structures to convey your information and explanation as clearly and engagingly as possible to the reader.

What do better writers do?

Better writers craft their sentences, selecting a variety of clauses and structures to convey information as clearly and engagingly as possible.

CHECK YOUR WRITING

➲ Look back at your writing in Activity 2 question 3 and at the table below. Which column do you think best describes your writing?

I tried to use some humour to engage and entertain the reader.	I used some humour to engage and entertain the reader.	I thought about the effect I wanted each part of my text to have on the reader, including humour in some parts to engage and entertain the reader.
I used some different sentence structures including simple sentences, coordinate and subordinate clauses.	I used a range of different sentence structures and chose some of them to convey information as accurately and clearly as possible.	I used a varied range of sentence structures, carefully selecting them to ensure I was conveying information as accurately and clearly as possible.

Learning objectives

- Understand how a writer can create an informal relationship with their reader, using informal language and sentence structure choices

- Understand the impact of register on the reader

Sometimes a text can entertain as well as inform and explain.

Activity 1

LARP stands for Live Action Role Play – a hobby in which people create the characters and events of a fantasy game and bring its world to life.

Read the article below about the hobby of 'Larping'.

We could be heroes

To an outsider, the world of the Larper just isn't right. Superficially, it's a bunch of guys in fancy dress running around hitting each other with rubber swords. On closer inspection, though, you see there's girls doing it too. 'Why can't they just watch telly like the rest of us?' you cry. But they're not listening, **ensconced** as they are in email debates about the **barbarian insurgency** and 'what splatters best, ketchup or jam?'

Oh yes, it's all too easy to laugh at a Larper. But there's an estimated 20,000 players in the UK alone. So what's the appeal? For journalist Ed Fortune it's simple: 'Larping fires the imagination. It's like playing 'let's pretend' when you're a kid. We've simply chosen not to grow out of that. And now we've got better toys.'

On a windswept Friday night I head to a 200-year-old fort on the slopes above **Pompey**. As a child I used to go sledging on these hills. What surprises do they hold now? Will it be Gandalf waiting for me? In the end, it's a bloke called Chris.

As co-writer and ref of Oblivion, Chris spends the weekend dashing around the fort, ensuring fair or foul play, and moving things along with clues and interventions. He's assisted by three other refs and a team of 20 'monsters' (non-player characters and behind-the-scenes people). Together they make the whole adventure happen.

Everywhere I look over the weekend there are strange things afoot. On Saturday, a bunch of mercenaries take a boat out into the harbour. Unfortunately, there's no water, so they have to pretend to row a vaguely boat-shaped wooden frame across a dry, grassy moat. Then they get hit by a tidal wave (an oversize plastic sheet dragged across their ducking heads), before fending off a sea beast (five-metre plastic 'tentacles' waggled provocatively at them by the monster team). As a spectacle it's both ridiculous and hilarious, yet totally compelling.

'Of course people take the mick,' says Thaddeus (Matt, an IT analyst). 'But there's not many hobbies that can give you this much of a buzz.' Which explains why players have come down here from as far as Liverpool and Wales. And it's not just the computer nerds. There's an art director, policeman, photographer... a bit of everything really – and 20 or so girls.

So the players get to dress up, take on a whole new personality and, let's not forget, hit each other, but what's in it for the refs and monsters? 'There's a real satisfaction when people are enjoying it,' explains Chris. 'If you've got it right, they forget their humdrum lives. We write the story to try to draw out people's best points, so that, for a moment in time, they can be a hero.'

1 a Write down two pieces of information which this text has given you.

   b Write down two things which the writer of this text has explained to you.

2 a What impression does the article give you of Larping? Choose a quotation or two to support your ideas.

   b Sum up the writer's opinion of Larping in one or two sentences. Choose a quotation or two to support your ideas.

Glossary

ensconced: absorbed, engrossed

barbarian insurgency: a rebellion by barbarians, intended to overthrow a monarch or government; in this article, a reference to an event in a LARP game

Pompey: nickname for Portsmouth

83

WRITER'S WORKSHOP: Sounding the right note

Why would I want to use informal, colloquial language in an explanation text?

You have already looked at some information and explanation texts which use formal language and the third person to create the impression that they are reliable and accurate. However, the writer of the text on page 82 does neither.

He uses the first person.

> On a windswept Friday night (I) head to a 200-year-old fort on the slopes above Pompey.

He uses informal language.

> Superficially, it's a bunch of guys in fancy dress running around hitting each other with rubber swords.

He uses informal sentence structures.

> But there's an estimated 20,000 players in the UK alone.

The writer starts the sentence with a coordinating conjunction.

He uses colloquial language (which means it sounds like a casual conversation with the reader).

> Oh yes, it's all too easy to laugh at a Larper.

And he contrasts this informal, colloquial language with more formal, sophisticated language to create humour.

informal sentence structure   formal, sophisticated language choice

> But they're not listening, ensconced as they are in email debates about the barbarian insurgency and 'what splatters best, ketchup or jam?'

formal, sophisticated language choice   informal language choice, colloquial sentence structure

Choose three or four sentences from the article on page 82. Try rewriting them in the third person, using much more formal language. What effect have your changes had on the tone of the text?

Activity 2

1 Look again at the writing you completed in Activity 2 on page 81: the opening paragraphs to an article on the unusual sport of rabbit show jumping.

Write the next two paragraphs of your article. Aim to create humour and an intimate relationship with your reader by:

• writing in the first person
• choosing more informal or colloquial language and sentence structures
• contrasting formal and informal language.

What do better writers do?

Better writers select language and sentence structure to achieve a specific tone or register in their writing, depending on the relationship they want to create with their reader.

• More formal language and sentence structure choices create an impression of authority.
• More informal language and sentence structure creates a more intimate, almost friendly relationship in which the writer shares their thoughts and experiences with the reader.

Better writers can manipulate the tone of their writing for specific effect – for example, contrasting colloquial and sophisticated language choices to create humour.

CHECK YOUR WRITING

Looking at the table below, decide which column you think best describes your writing in Activity 2.

I wrote my article in the first person and used some informal language.	I tried to create a more informal relationship with my reader by writing in the first person, and by using some colloquial language and sentence structures.	I crafted my writing to create an informal relationship with my reader, using colloquial language and sentence structures, and contrasting them with more formal language choices to create humour.

11 Planning a complete text

Learning objective

- Understand how to plan a web article which informs, explains and entertains

Your final task in this unit will be to write an article which informs, explains and entertains. Before you can start writing, you need to gather your ideas. Use the activities on these pages to help you plan your writing.

Activity 1

1 You have received the following email from the editor of a website.

Before you can write your article, you need to think which unusual sport or hobby you could write about.

You could find out more about one of the strange activities listed below ... or you could invent a new and unusual sport or hobby.

INBOX   [reply] [reply all] [forward] [X delete]

From
To
Subject

Dear Writer

We need an article for the website. We're looking for a piece of writing about an unusual sport or hobby, about 500–1000 words, which should inform and explain all about your chosen subject to the reader, while keeping them engaged and entertained.

Man v horse: a 22-mile marathon in Wales in which humans compete against horses

Unicycle hockey: like street hockey, but all the players are riding unicycles

Bog snorkelling: contestants swim 55 metres through a bog wearing a snorkel

Gurning: contestants try to pull the ugliest face they can, while wearing a horse collar

Toe wrestling: like arm wrestling ... but with toes

Competitive dog grooming: using vegetable dye and clippers, dog owners sculpt their pet's fur into a fancy-dress outfit

Guerrilla gardening: gardeners find a piece of unloved, untended land and make it beautiful under cover of darkness

2 a Now you have chosen your subject, you need to gather some ideas for your article. Imagine you have spent a day with people who take part in your chosen (or imagined) sport or hobby.

- How did you spend your day?
- Who did you meet? What did you ask them? What did they tell you?
- What did you see and hear?
- What did you find out?
- What would your readers want to know about this sport or hobby?
- What would your readers need to have explained? For example, how is this sport played? Why do people enjoy it?

b Plan your article, thinking about how you will tell the story of your day, and combine it with information and explanations about your chosen sport or hobby. You could note down your ideas in a table like the one below.

Paragraph	The story	Information/explanation
1		
2		
3		

Activity 2

You now need to think about some of the writing choices you might make in your article. Answer the questions below to help you.

1 Will you write in the first person or the third person?

2 Will you use the past tense or the present tense? The events you describe will have already happened, but using the present tense could help to engage the reader.

3 Will you use the passive voice at any point in your writing? Or will you only use the active voice?

4 How will you develop your simple sentences with adjectives and adverbial phrases to convey information to the reader?

5 How will you use a range of other sentence structures, including coordinate clauses, subordinate clauses, relative clauses and non-finite clauses, to convey information as clearly and concisely as possible?

6 Will you use formal or informal language and sentence structures? Or will you use a mixture of both for effect?

What do better writers do?

Better writers:

- consider the effect they want their text to have on the reader – and how they will achieve that effect
- plan their writing, selecting key ideas and information to make their writing as interesting and engaging as possible
- think about and plan the language and sentence structures they will use to achieve their intended purpose and tone.

CHECK YOUR PLANNING

→ Look at all the planning for your story. Will the article you have planned:

- inform the reader about your chosen sport or hobby
- explain how and why people want to take part in it
- engage and entertain the reader from start to finish?

→ If you answered 'Maybe', 'I hope so' or 'No' to any of these questions, have another think about your plan and what you can do to improve it.

Assessment: Writing to explain and inform

Learning objective

- Understand how to write a web article which informs, explains and entertains

WRITE

You are now ready to complete the final task in this unit.

Remember to:

- follow the plan you prepared on pages 86 and 87
- use all the skills and knowledge you have gained and practised in this unit
- think about the decisions you need to make as a writer
- inform, explain, entertain.

reply | reply all | forward | X delete

From
To
Subject

Dear Writer

We need an article for the website. We're looking for a piece of writing about an unusual sport or hobby, about 500–1000 words, which should inform and explain all about your chosen subject to the reader, while keeping them engaged and entertained.

REFLECT

1. When you have finished writing the first draft of your article, read it through carefully. Are you pleased with it? Which of these statements do you feel you have achieved – and which could you improve?

   For each of the statements you feel you have achieved, write a sentence explaining the effect and impact of your choices.

   - ☐ I think my choice of writing in the first or third person is effective.
   - ☐ I think my choice of past or present tense is effective.
   - ☐ I think I have used the active and passive voices effectively in my writing.
   - ☐ I think I have used a range of sentence structures in my writing.
   - ☐ I think I have achieved an effective tone or register in my writing.
   - ☐ I think I have given the reader lots of information about my chosen sport or hobby.
   - ☐ I think I have explained everything that the reader needs to understand about my chosen sport or hobby.

2. a Choose one or two areas in your writing which you feel you could improve. This might be:

   - making more use of a particular choice in your writing, such as

   > using more formal language to contrast with the informal language I have used

   - or improving a particular section of your writing, such as

   > using more developed simple sentences to inform the reader about my chosen sport or hobby more clearly in the first paragraph.

   b Working on your own, or with a partner, look back at the relevant pages in this unit to remind yourself of the choices you would make to improve your writing in those one or two areas.

   c Write a sentence or two explaining how you will improve your writing in those one or two areas.

   d Make the improvements you want to make to your writing.

CHECK YOUR WRITING

1 Put on your teacher's hat and mark your own work. Using a different coloured pen (if your story is handwritten) or the comments feature (if your story is word-processed), annotate and explain some of your successes.

It might look something like this:

> Opening simple sentences developed with adjectives and adverbial phrases create an engaging scene

I am waiting patiently in a cold, draughty sports hall. An enthusiastic crowd is slowly building to a crescendo of excitement. Four men on bicycles and a football roll into the arena. The game of cycle ball is about to begin.

> First person and present tense suggest events happening as the reader reads

> Series of coordinate clauses describes a sequence of events

I ask the woman next to me why she has come to watch this strange game today. Her husband is one of the players, she tells me, pointing at him. He wobbles on his bike, begins to topple and finally crashes to the ground. She screams and calls out to him. He gets up, picks up his bike and smiles, pretending not to care.

2 Looking at the table below, decide which column you think best describes the writing you crafted in this assessment.

I planned and wrote my article thinking about how I could inform and engage the reader.	I planned and wrote my article thinking about how it would inform and entertain the reader.	I planned and wrote my article thinking carefully about the effect that the information and events I included would have on the reader.
I chose some of the language in my article thinking about the effect I wanted to have on the reader.	I used quite a wide vocabulary which I chose thinking about the tone I wanted to create.	I used a varied range of vocabulary which I chose thinking about the tone and the relationship with the reader that I wanted to create.
I tried to use a variety of sentence structures.	I used a range of sentence structures and chose some of them to convey information and explanations as accurately and clearly as possible.	I used a varied range of sentence structures, sometimes to convey information and explanations as accurately and clearly as possible and sometimes to create a specific tone and relationship with the reader.
	I used the active and passive voices.	I used the active voice mainly, and the passive voice to achieve a more formal tone or to direct the reader's attention to key information.